Oedipus

the King

P9-AZX-011

ALSO BY ROBERT BAGG

Madonna of the Cello: Poems (Wesleyan University Press)

Euripides' Hippolytos (Oxford University Press)

The Scrawny Sonnets and Other Narratives
(Illinois University Press)

Euripides' The Bakkhai (University of Massachusetts Press)

Sophocles' Oedipus the King
(University of Massachusetts Press)

Body Blows: Poems New and Selected
(University of Massachusetts Press)

The Oedipus Plays of Sophocles with Notes and Introductions by
Robert and Mary Bagg (University of Massachusetts Press)

Niké and Other Poems (Azul Editions)

HORSEGOD: Collected Poems (iUniverse)

Euripides III: Hippolytos and Other Plays
(Oxford University Press)

The Tandem Ride and Other Excursions
(Spiritus Mundi Press)

The Complete Plays of Sophocles with James Scully
(Harper Perennial)

The Oedipus Cycle
(Harper Perennial)

OEDIPUS THE KING

A New Translation by Robert Bagg

SOPHOCLES

HARPER PERENNIAL

NEW YORK • LONDON • TORONTO • SYDNEY • NEW DELHI • AUCKLAND

HARPER PERENNIAL

For performance rights to *Oedipus the King* contact The Strothman Agency, LLC, at 197 Eighth Street, Flagship Wharf – 611, Charlestown, MA 02129, or by email at info@strothmanagency.com.

OEDIPUS THE KING. Copyright © 2004, 2012 by Robert Bagg. "When Theater Was Life: The World of Sophocles" copyright © 2011 by Robert Bagg and James Scully. All rights reserved. Printed in the United States of America. No part of this book may be used or reproduced in any manner whatsoever without written permission except in the case of brief quotations embodied in critical articles and reviews. For information, address HarperCollins Publishers, 195 Broadway, New York, NY 10007.

HarperCollins books may be purchased for educational, business, or sales promotional use. For information, please e-mail the Special Markets Department at SPsales@harpercollins.com.

FIRST EDITION

Designed by Justin Dodd

Library of Congress Cataloging-in-Publication Data is available upon request.

ISBN 978-0-06-213208-6

22 23 24 25 26 LBC 15 14 13 12 11

For Teresa Choate, with thanks for her memorable production of Oedipus the King *on the concrete steps of the Parthenon in Nashville, Tennessee, in 1983*

CONTENTS

WHEN THEATER WAS LIFE: THE WORLD OF SOPHOCLES

I

Greek theater emerged from the same explosive creativity that propelled the institutions and ways of knowing of ancient Athens, through two and a half millennia, into our own era. These ranged from the concept and practice of democracy, to an aggressive use of logic with few holds barred, to a philosophy singing not of gods and heroes but of what exists, where it came from, and why. Athenians distinguished history from myth, acutely observed the human form, and reconceived medicine from a set of beliefs and untheorized practices into a science.

Playwrights, whose work was presented to audiences of thousands, effectively took center stage as critics and interpreters of their own culture. Athenian drama had one major showing each year at the nine-day Festival of Dionysos. It was rigorously vetted. Eight dramatists (three tragedians, five comic playwrights), chosen in open competition, were "granted choruses," a down-to-earth term meaning that the city financed production of their plays. For the Athenians theater was as central to civic life as the assembly, law courts, temples, and agora.

Historians summing up Athens' cultural importance have tended to emphasize its glories, attending less to the brutal institutions and policies that underwrote the city's wealth and dominance: its slaves, for instance, who worked the mines that enriched the communal treasury; or its policy of executing the men and enslaving the women and children of enemy cities that refused to surrender on demand. During its long war with Sparta, Athens' raw and unbridled democracy became increasingly reckless, cruel, and eventually self-defeating. Outside the assembly's daily debates on war, peace, and myriad other issues, Athenian citizens, most notably the indefatigable Socrates, waged ongoing critiques of the city's actions and principles. Playwrights, whom the Athenians called *didaskaloi* (educators), were expected to enlighten audiences about themselves, both individually and collectively. As evidenced by the thirty-three plays that survive, these works presented a huge audience annually with conflicts and dilemmas of the most extreme sort.

To some extent all Sophocles' plays engage personal, social, and political crises and confrontations—not just those preserved in heroic legend but those taking place in his immediate world. Other Athenian intellectuals, including Thucydides, Aeschylus, Euripides, Plato, and Aristophanes, were part of that open-ended discussion in which everything was subject to question, including the viability of the city and its democracy (which was twice voted temporarily out of existence).

II

To this day virtually every Athenian theatrical innovation—from paraphernalia such as scenery, costumes, and masks to the architecture of stage and seating and, not least, to the use of drama as a powerful means of cultural and political commentary—remains in use. We thus inherit from Athens the vital *potential* for drama to engage our realities and to support or critique prevailing orthodoxies.

The myths that engaged Sophocles' audience originated in Homer's epics of the Trojan War and its aftermath. Yet Homer's world was tribal. That of the Greek tragedians was not, or only nominally so. With few exceptions (e.g., Aeschylus' *The Persians*), those playwrights were writing *through* the Homeric world to address, and deal with, the *polis* world they themselves were living in. Sophocles was appropriating stories and situations from these epics, which were central to the mythos of Athenian culture, and re-visioning them into dramatic *agons* (contests) relevant to the tumultuous, often vicious politics of Greek life in the fifth century BCE. Today some of Sophocles' concerns, and the way he approached them, correspond at their deepest levels to events and patterns of thought and conduct that trouble our own time. For example, "[Sophocles'] was an age when war was endemic. And Athens in the late fifth century BC appeared to have a heightened taste for conflict. One year of two in the Democratic Assembly, Athenian citizens voted in favor of military aggression" (Hughes, 138).

Each generation interprets and translates these plays in keeping with the style and idiom it believes best suited for tragedy.

Inevitably even the most skilled at preserving the original's essentials, while attuning its voice to the present, will eventually seem the relic of a bygone age. We have assumed that a contemporary translation should attempt to convey not only what the original seems to have been communicating, but *how* it communicated—not in its saying, only, but in its *doing*. It cannot be said too often: these plays were social and historical *events* witnessed by thousands in a context and setting infused with religious ritual and civic protocol. They were not transitory, one-off entertainments but were preserved, memorized, and invoked. Respecting this basic circumstance will not guarantee a successful translation, but it is a precondition for giving these works breathing room in which their strangeness, their rootedness in distinct historical moments, can flourish. As with life itself, they were not made of words alone.

Athenian playwrights relied on a settled progression of scene types: usually a prologue followed by conversations or exchanges in which situations and attitudes are introduced, then a series of confrontations that feature cut-and-thrust dialogue interrupted by messenger narratives, communal songs of exultation or grieving, and less emotionally saturated, or 'objective,' choral odes that respond to or glance off the action. Audiences expected chorus members to be capable of conveying the extraordinary range of expressive modes, from the pithy to the operatic, that Sophocles had at his disposal. To translate this we have needed the resources not only of idiomatic English but also of rhetorical gravitas and, on occasion, colloquial English. Which is why we have adopted, regarding vocabulary and 'levels of speech,' a wide and varied palette. When Philoktetes

exclaims, "You said it, boy," that saying corresponds in character to the colloquial Greek expression. On the other hand Aias's
"Long rolling waves of time . . ." is as elevated, without being
pompous, as anything can be.

Unfortunately we've been taught, and have learned to live
with, washed-out stereotypes of the life and art of 'classical'
times—just as we have come to associate Greek sculpture with
the color of its underlying material, usually white marble. The
classical historian Bettany Hughes writes in *The Hemlock Cup*
(81) that temples and monuments were painted or stained in
"Technicolor" to be seen under the bright Attic sun. The stat-
ues' eyes were not blanks gazing off into space. They had color:
a *look*. To restore their flesh tones, their eye color, and the
bright hues of their cloaks would seem a desecration. We should
understand that this is so—even as we recognize that, for us,
there is no going back. We've been conditioned to preserve not
the reality of ancient Greek sculpture in its robust cultural am-
bience and physical setting, but our own fixed conception of it
as colorless and sedate—a perception created, ironically, by the
weathering and ravages of centuries. No one can change that.
Still, as translators we have a responsibility not to reissue a ste-
reotype of classical Greek culture but rather to recoup, to the
extent possible, the vitality of its once living reality.

Regarding its highly inflected language, so different from our
more context-driven modern English, we recognize that locu-
tions sounding contorted, coy, recondite, or annoyingly round-
about were a feature of ordinary Greek and were intensified in
theatrical discourse. Highly wrought, larger-than-life expressions, delivered without artificial amplification to an audience

of thousands, did not jar when resonating in the vast Theater of
Dionysos, but may to our own Anglophone ears when delivered
from our more intimate stages and screens, or read in our books
and electronic tablets. Accordingly, where appropriate, and especially in rapid exchanges, we have our characters speak more
straightforwardly—as happens in Greek stichomythia, when
characters argue back and forth in alternating lines (or 'rows')
of verse, usually linked by a word they hold in common. Here,
for example, is a snippet from *Aias* (1305–1309)[1] that pivots on
"right," "killer," "dead" and "god(s)":

TEUKROS   A righteous cause is my courage.
MENELAOS What? It's right to defend my killer?
TEUKROS   Your killer!? You're dead? And still alive?
MENELAOS A god saved me. But he *wanted* me dead.
TEUKROS   If the gods saved you, why disrespect them?

There are no rules for determining when a more-literal or
less-literal approach is appropriate. Historical and dramatic
context have to be taken into account. The objective is not
only to render the textual meaning (which is ordinarily more
on the phrase-by-phrase than the word-by-word level) but also
to communicate the feel and impact embedded in that meaning. Dictionaries are indispensable for translators, but they are
not sufficient. The meanings of words are immeasurably more
nuanced and wide-ranging in life than they can ever be in a
lexicon. As in life, where most 'sayings' cannot be fully grasped
apart from their timing and their place in both personal and
social contexts, so in theater: dramatic context must take words

up and finish them off. In *Aias*, Teukros, the out-of-wedlock half brother of Aias, and Menelaos, co-commander of the Greek forces, are trading insults. When Menelaos says, "The archer, far from blood dust, thinks he's something," Teukros quietly rejoins, "I'm very good at what I do" (1300–1301).

Understanding the exchange between the two men requires that the reader or audience recognize the 'class' implications of archery. Socially and militarily, archers rank low in the pecking order. They stand to the rear of the battle formation. Archers are archers usually because they can't afford the armor one needs to be a hoplite, a frontline fighter. The point is that Teukros refuses to accept 'his place' in the social and military order. For a Greek audience, the sheer fact of standing his ground against a commander had to have been audacious. But that is not how it automatically registers in most modern word-by-word translations, which tend to make Teukros sound defensive (a trait wholly out of his character in this play). Examples: (a) "Even so, 'tis no sordid craft that I possess," (b) "I'm not the master of a menial skill," (c) "My archery is no contemptible science," (d) "The art I practice is no mean one." These translations are technically accurate. They're scrupulous in reproducing the Greek construction whereby, in an idiomatic context, a negative may register as an assertion—or even, framed as a negative future question, become a command. But tonally, in modern English idiom, Teukros' negation undercuts his assertion (the 'I'm not . . . but even so' formula). To our ears it admits weakness or defensiveness. "I'm very good at what I do," however, is a barely veiled threat. The dramatic arc of the encounter, which confirms that Teukros will not back down for anything or anyone, not even a commander of the Greek army, substantiates that Sophocles meant it to be heard as such.

Hearing the line in context we realize instantly not only what the words are saying but, more pointedly and feelingly, what they're doing. His words are not just 'about' something. They are an act in themselves—not, as in the more literal translations, a duress-driven apologia. Translation must thus respond to an individual character's ever-changing demeanor and circumstance. The speaker's state of mind should show through his or her words, just as in life. Idiomatic or colloquial expressions fit many situations better—especially those that have a more finely tuned emotional economy—than phrases that, if uninhabited, hollowed out, or just plain buttoned-up, sound evasive or euphemistic. Many of the speeches Sophocles gives his characters are as abrupt and common as he might himself have spoken to his fellow Athenians in the assembly, in the agora, to his troops, his actors, or his family.

At times we have chosen a more literal translation in passages where scholars have opted for a seemingly more accessible modern phrase. At the climactic moment in *Oedipus the King*, when Oedipus realizes he has killed his father and fathered children with his mother, he says in a modern prose version by Hugh Lloyd-Jones: "Oh, oh! All is now clear. O light, may I now look on you for the last time, I who am revealed as cursed in my birth, cursed in my marriage, cursed in my killing!" (Greek 1182–1885). When Lloyd-Jones uses and repeats the word "cursed," he is compressing a longer Greek phrase meaning "being shown to have done what must not be done." This compression shifts the emphasis from his unsuspecting human

actions toward the realm of the god who acted to "curse" him.
The following lines keep the original grammatical construction:

> All! All! It has all happened!
> It was all true. O light! Let this
> be the last time I look on you.
> You see now who I am—
> the child who must not be born!
> I loved where I must not love!
> I killed where I must not kill! (1336–1342)

Here Oedipus names the three acts of interfamilial transgression that it was both his good and his ill fortune to have
survived, participated in, and inflicted—birth, sexual love, and
murder in self-defense—focusing not only on the curse each act
has become but now realizing the full and horrific consequence
of each action that was, as it happened, unknowable. Registering the shudder rushing through him, Oedipus's exclamations
convey the shock of his realization: *I did these things without
feeling their horror as I do now.*

Finally, translations tend to be more or less effective depending on their ability to convey the emotional and physiological
reactions that will give a reader or an audience a kinesthetic relationship to the dramatic moment, whether realized as text or
performance. This is a precondition for maintaining the tactility that characterizes any living language. Dante wrote that the
spirit of poetry abounds "in the tangled constructions and defective pronunciations" of vernacular speech where language is
renewed and transformed. We have not attempted that—these

are translations, not new works—but we have striven for a language that is spontaneous and generative as opposed to one that is studied and bodiless. We have also worked to preserve the root meaning of Sophocles' Greek, especially his always illuminating metaphors.

III

Sophocles reveals several recurrent attitudes in his plays—sympathy for fate's victims, hostility toward leaders who abuse their power, skepticism toward self-indulgent 'heroes,' disillusionment with war and revenge—that are both personal and politically significant. All his plays to a greater or lesser degree focus on outcasts from their communities. Historically, those who transgress a community's values have either been physically exiled or stigmatized by sanctions and/or shunning. To keep a polity from breaking apart, everyone, regardless of social standing, must abide by certain enforceable communal expectations. Athens in the fifth century BCE practiced political ostracism, a procedure incorporated in its laws. By voting to ostracize a citizen, Athens withdrew its protection and civic benefits—sometimes to punish an offender, but also as a kind of referee's move, expelling a divisive public figure from the city (and from his antagonists) so as to promote a ten-year period of relative peace.

In earlier eras Greek cities also cast out those who committed sacrilege. Murderers of kin, for instance, or blasphemers of a god—in myth and in real life—were banished from Greek cities until the 'unclean' individual 'purged' his crime according to current religious custom. The imperative to banish a kin violator runs so deep that Oedipus, after discovering he has committed patricide and incest, passes judgment on himself and demands to live in exile. In *Oedipus at Kolonos*, he and Antigone have been exiled from Thebes against their will. In the non-Oedipus plays the title characters Philoktetes, Elektra, and Aias, as well as Herakles in *Women of Trakhis*, are not outcasts in the traditional sense, though all have actively or involuntarily offended their social units in some way. They may or may not be typical tragic characters; nonetheless none 'fit' the world they're given to live in. In these translations we've incorporated awareness of social dimensions in the original texts, which, as they involve exercises of power, are no less political than social.

In each of the four non-Oedipus plays, a lethal confrontation or conflict 'crazes' the surface coherence of a society (presumed to be Athenian society, either in itself or as mediated through a military context), thus revealing and heightening its internal contradictions.

In *Women of Trakhis* the revered hero Herakles, when he tries to impose a young concubine on his wife Deianeira, provokes her to desperate measures that unwittingly cause him horrific pain, whereupon he exposes his savage and egomaniacal nature, lashing out at everyone around him, exercising a hero's prerogatives so savagely that he darkens his own reputation and drives his wife to suicide and his son to bitter resentment.

Elektra exposes the dehumanizing cost of taking revenge, by revealing the neurotic, materialistic, and cold-blooded character of the avengers. In *Aias*, when the Greek Army's most powerful soldier tries to assassinate his commanders, whose authority rests on dubious grounds, he exposes not only them but his own growing obsolescence in a prolonged war that has more need of strategic acumen, as exemplified by Odysseus, than brute force. In *Philoktetes* the title character, abandoned on a deserted island because of a stinking wound his fellow warriors can't live with, is recalled to active service with the promise of a cure and rehabilitation. The army needs him and his bow to win the war. It is a call he resists, until the god Herakles negotiates a resolution—not in the name of justice, but because Philoktetes' compliance is culturally mandated. As in *Aias*, the object is to maintain the integrity and thus the survival of the society itself. The greatest threat is not an individual's death, which here is not the preeminent concern, but the disintegration of a society.

In our own time aspects of *Aias* and *Philoktetes* have been used for purposes that Sophocles, who was the sponsor in Athens of a healing cult, might have appreciated. Both heroes, but especially Aias, have been appropriated as exemplars of post-traumatic stress disorder, in particular as suffered by soldiers in and out of a war zone. Excerpts from these two plays have been performed around the United States for veterans, soldiers on active duty, their families, and concerned others. Ultimately, however, Sophocles is intent on engaging and resolving internal contradictions that threaten the historical continuity, the very future, of the Athenian city-state. He invokes the class contradictions Athens was experiencing by applying them to the mythical/historical eras from which he draws his plots.

Modern-day relevancies implicit in Sophocles' plays will come sharply into focus or recede from view depending on time and circumstance. The constant factors in these plays will always be their consummate poetry, dramatic propulsion, and the intensity with which they illuminate human motivation and morality. Scholars have also identified allusions in his plays to events in Athenian history. The plague in *Oedipus the King* is described in detail so vivid it dovetails in many respects with Thucydides' more clinical account of the plague that killed one-third to one-half of Athens' population beginning in 429 BCE. Kreon, Antigone's antagonist, displays the imperviousness to rational advice and lack of foresight exhibited by the politicians of Sophocles' era, whose follies Thucydides narrates, and which Sophocles himself was called in to help repair—specifically by taking a democracy that in a fit of imperial overreach suffered, in 413, a catastrophic defeat on the shores of Sicily, and replacing it with a revanchist oligarchy. When Pisander, one of the newly empowered oligarchs, asked Sophocles if he was one of the councilors who had approved the replacement of the democratic assembly by what was, in effect, a junta of four hundred, Sophocles admitted that he had. "Why?" asked Pisander. "Did you not think this a terrible decision?" Sophocles agreed it was. "So weren't you doing something terrible?" "That's right. There was no better alternative." (Aristotle, Rh. 1419a). The lesson? When life, more brutally than drama, delivers its irreversible calamities and judgments, it forces a polity, most movingly, to an utterly unanticipated, wholly 'other' moral and spiritual level.

In *Oedipus at Kolonos* Sophocles alludes to his city's decline when he celebrates a self-confident Athens that no longer existed when Sophocles wrote that play. He gives us Theseus, a throwback to the type of thoughtful, decisive, all-around leader Athens lacked as it pursued policies that left it impoverished

and defenseless—this under the delusion that its only enemies
were Spartans and Sparta's allies.

IV

Archaeologists have identified scores of local theaters all over
the Greek world—stone semicircles, some in cities and at religious destinations, others in rural villages. Within many of
these structures both ancient and modern plays are still staged.
Hillsides whose slopes were wide and gentle enough to seat a
crowd made perfect settings for dramatic encounters and were
the earliest theaters. Ancient roads that widened below a gentle
hillside, or level ground at a hill's base, provided suitable performance spaces. Such sites, along with every city's agora and
a temple dedicated to Dionysos or another god, were the main
arenas of community activity. Stone tablets along roads leading
to theaters commemorated local victors: athletes, actors, playwrights, singers, and the winning plays' producers. Theaters,
in every sense, were open to all the crosscurrents of civic and
domestic life.

    The components of the earliest theaters reflect their rural
origins and were later incorporated into urban settings. *The-
atron*, the root of our word "theater," translates as "viewing
place" and designated the curved and banked seating area.
Orchestra was literally "the place for dancing." The costumed
actors emerged from and retired to the *skenê*, a word that origi-
nally meant, and literally was in the rural theaters, a tent. As
theaters evolved to become more permanent structures, the
skenê developed as well into a "stage building" whose painted

facade changed, like a mask, with the characters' various habitats. Depending on the drama, the *skenê* could assume the appearance of a king's grand palace, the Kyklops' cave, a temple to a god, or (reverting to its original material form) an army commander's tent.

Greek drama itself originated in two earlier traditions, one rural, one civic. Choral singing of hymns to honor Dionysos or other gods and heroes, which had begun in the countryside, evolved into the structured choral ode. The costumes and the dancing of choral singers, often accompanied by a reed instrument, are depicted on sixth-century vases that predate the plays staged in the Athenian theater. The highly confrontational nature of every play suggests how early choral odes and dialogues came into being in concert with a fundamental aspect of democratic governance: public and spirited debate. Two or more characters facing off in front of an audience was a situation at the heart of both drama and democratic politics.

Debate, the democratic Athenian art practiced and perfected by politicians, litigators, and thespians—relished and judged by voters, juries, and audiences—flourished in theatrical venues and permeated daily Athenian life. Thucydides used it to narrate his history of the war between Athens and Sparta. He recalled scores of lengthy debates that laid out the motives of politicians, generals, and diplomats as each argued his case for a particular policy or a strategy. Plato, recognizing the open-ended, exploratory power of spirited dialogue, wrote his philosophy entirely in dramatic form.

The Greeks were addicted to contests and turned virtually every chance for determining a winner into a formal competition. The Great Dionysia for playwrights and choral singers and the Olympics for athletes are only the most famous and familiar. The verbal *agon* remains to this day a powerful medium for testing and judging issues. And character, as in the debate between Teukros and Menelaos, may be laid bare. But there is no guarantee. Persuasiveness can be, and frequently is, manipulative (e.g., many of the sophists evolved into hired rhetorical guns, as distinguished from the truth-seeking, pre-Socratic philosophers). Sophocles may well have had the sophists' amorality in mind when he had Odysseus persuade Neoptomolos that betraying Philoktetes would be a patriotic act and bring the young man fame.

Though they were part of a high-stakes competition, the plays performed at the Dionysia were part of a religious ceremony whose chief purpose was to honor theater's patron god, Dionysos. The god's worshippers believed that Dionysos' powers and rituals transformed the ways in which they experienced and dealt with their world—from their enthralled response to theatrical illusion and disguise to the exhilaration, liberation, and violence induced by wine. Yet the festival also aired, or licensed, civic issues that might otherwise have had no truly public, *polis*-wide expression. The playwrights wrote as *politai*, civic poets, as distinguished from those who focused on personal lyrics and shorter choral works. Though *Aias* and *Philoktetes* are set in a military milieu, the issues they engage are essentially civil and political. Neither *Aias* nor *Philoktetes* is concerned with the 'enemy of record,' Troy, but rather with Greek-on-Greek conflict. With civil disruption, and worse. In fact one need look no further than the play venue itself for confirmation of the interpenetration of the civic with the military—a concern bordering on preoccupation—when, every year, the orphans of warriors killed in battle were given new hoplite armor and a place of honor at the Festival of Dionysos.

Communal cohesiveness and the historical continuity of the polity are most tellingly threatened from within: in *Aias* by the individualistic imbalance and arrogance of Aias, whose warrior qualities and strengths are also his weakness—they lead him to destroy the war spoil that is the common property of the entire Greek army—and in *Philoktetes* by the understandable and just, yet inordinately unyielding, self-preoccupation of Philoktetes himself. In both cases the fundamental, encompassing question is this: With what understandings, what basic values, is the commonality of the *polis* to be recovered and rededicated in an era in which civic cohesiveness is under the extreme pressure of a war Athens is losing (especially at the time *Philoktetes* was produced) and, further, the simmering stasis of unresolved class or caste interests? In sharply different ways, all three plays of the Oedipus cycle, as well as *Aias* and *Elektra*, cast doubt on the legitimacy of usurped, authoritarian, or publicly disapproved leadership.

Given the historical and political dynamism of these great, instructive works, we've aimed to translate and communicate their challenge to Athenian values for a contemporary audience whose own values are no less under duress.

V

The Great Dionysia was the central and most widely attended event of the political year, scheduled after winter storms had abated so that foreign visitors could come and bear witness to Athens' wealth, civic pride, imperial power, and artistic imagination. For eight or nine days each spring, during the heyday of Greek theater in the fifth century BCE, Athenians flocked to the temple grounds sacred to Dionysos on the southern slope of the Acropolis. After dark on the first day, a parade of young men hefted a giant phallic icon of the god from the temple and into the nearby theater. As the icon had been festooned with garlands of ivy and a mask of the god's leering face, their raucous procession initiated a dramatic festival called the City Dionysia, a name that differentiated it from the festival's ancient rural origins in Dionysian myth and cult celebrations of the god. As the festival gained importance in the sixth century BCE, most likely through the policies of Pisistratus, it was also known as the Great Dionysia.

Pisistratus, an Athenian tyrant in power off and on beginning in 561 BCE and continuously from 546 to 527, had good reason for adapting the Rural Dionysia as Athens' Great Dionysia: "Dionysos was a god for the 'whole' of democratic Athens" (Hughes, 213). Everyone, regardless of political faction or social standing, could relate to the boisterous communal activities of the festival honoring Dionysos: feasting, wine drinking, dancing, singing, romping through the countryside, and performing or witnessing dithyrambs and more elaborate dramatic works. The Great Dionysia thus served to keep in check, if not transcend, internal factionalizing by giving all citizens a 'natural' stake in Athens—Athens not simply as a place but as a venerable polity with ancient cultural roots. To this end Pisistratus had imported from Eleutherai an ancient phallic representation of Dionysos, one that took several men to carry.

Lodged as it was in a temple on the outskirts of Athens, this bigger-than-life icon gave the relatively new, citified cult the sanctified air of hoary antiquity (Csapo and Slater, 103–104). Thus validated culturally, the Great Dionysia was secured as a host to reassert, and annually rededicate, Athens as a democratic polity. As Bettany Hughes notes in *The Hemlock Cup*, "to call Greek drama an 'art-form' is somewhat anachronistic. The Greeks (unlike many modern-day bureaucrats) didn't distinguish drama as 'art'—something separate from 'society,' 'politics,' [or] 'life.' Theater was fundamental to democratic Athenian business. . . . [In] the fifth century this was the place where Athenian democrats came to understand the very world they lived in" (Hughes, 213).

The occasion offered Athens the chance to display treasure exacted from subjugated 'allies' (or tributes others willingly brought to the stage) and to award gold crowns to citizens whose achievements Athens' leaders wished to honor. Theater attendance itself was closely linked to citizenship; local town councils issued free festival passes to citizens in good standing. The ten generals elected yearly to conduct Athens' military campaigns poured libations to Dionysos. The theater's bowl seethed with a heady, sometimes unruly brew of military, political, and religious energy.

Performances began at dawn and lasted well into the

afternoon. The 14,000 or more Athenians present watched in god knows what state of anticipation or anxiety. Whatever else it did to entertain, move, and awe, Athenian tragedy consistently exposed human vulnerability to the gods' malice and favoritism. Because the gods were potent realities to Athenian audiences, they craved and expected an overwhelming emotional, physically distressing experience. That expectation distinguishes the greater intensity with which Athenians responded to plays from our own less challenging, more routine and frequent encounters with drama. Athenians wept while watching deities punish the innocent or unlucky, a reaction that distressed Plato. In his *Republic*, rather than question the motives or morality of the all-powerful Olympian gods for causing mortals grief, he blamed the poets and playwrights for their unwarranted wringing of the audience's emotions. He held that the gods had no responsibility for human suffering. True to form, Plato banned both poets and playwrights from his ideal city.

Modern audiences would be thoroughly at home with other, more cinematic stage effects. The sights and sounds tragedy delivered in the Theater of Dionysos were often spectacular. Aristotle, who witnessed a lifetime of productions in the fourth century—well after Sophocles' own lifetime, when the plays were performed in the heat of their historical moment—identified "spectacle," or *opsis*, as one of the basic (though to him suspect) elements of tragic theater. Under the influence of Aristotle, who preferred the study to the stage, and who therefore emphasized the poetry rather than the production of works, ancient commentators tended to consider "the visual aspects of drama [as] both vulgar and archaic" (Csapo and Slater, 257).

Nonetheless, visual and aural aspects there were: oboe music; dancing and the singing of set-piece odes by a chorus; masks that transformed the same male actor, for instance, into a swarthy-faced young hero, a dignified matron, Argos with a hundred eyes, or the Kyklops with only one. The theater featured painted scenery and large-scale constructions engineered with sliding platforms and towering cranes. It's hardly surprising that Greek tragedy has been considered a forerunner of Italian opera.

Judges awarding prizes at the Great Dionysia were chosen by lot from a list supplied by the council—one judge from each of Athens' ten tribes. Critical acumen was not required to get one's name on the list, but the *choregoi* (the producers and financial sponsors of the plays) were present when the jury was assembled and probably had a hand in its selection. At the conclusion of the festival the ten selected judges, each having sworn that he hadn't been bribed or unduly influenced, would inscribe on a tablet the names of the three competing playwrights in descending order of merit. The rest of the process depended on chance. The ten judges placed their ballots in a large urn. The presiding official drew five at random, counted up the weighted vote totals, and declared the winner.

VI

When Sophocles was a boy, masters trained him to excel in music, dance, and wrestling. He won crowns competing against his age-mates in all three disciplines. Tradition has it that he first appeared in Athenian national life at age fifteen, dancing naked (according to one source) and leading other boy dancers in a hymn of gratitude to celebrate Athens' defeat of the Persian fleet in the straits of Salamis.

Sophocles' father, Sophroniscus, manufactured weapons and armor (probably in a factory operated by slaves), and his mother, Phaenarete, was a midwife. The family lived in Kolonos, a rural suburb just north of Athens. Although his parents were not aristocrats, as most other playwrights' were, they surely had money and owned property; thus their status did not hamper their son's career prospects. Sophocles' talents as a dramatist, so formidable and so precociously developed, won him early fame. As an actor he triumphed in his own now-lost play, *Nausicaä*, in the role of the eponymous young princess who discovers the nearly naked Odysseus washed up on the beach while playing ball with her girlfriends.

During Sophocles' sixty-five-year career as a *didaskalos* he wrote and directed more than 120 plays and was awarded first prize at least eighteen times. No record exists of his placing lower than second. Of the seven entire works of his that survive, along with a substantial fragment of a satyr play, *The Trackers*, only two very late plays can be given exact production dates: *Philoktetes* in 409 and *Oedipus at Kolonos*, staged posthumously in 401. Some evidence suggests that *Antigone* was produced around 442–441 and *Oedipus the King* in the 420s. *Aias*, *Elektra*, and *Women of Trakhis* have been conjecturally, but never conclusively, dated through stylistic analysis. Aristotle, who had access we forever lack to the hundreds of fifth-century plays produced at the Dionysia, preferred Sophocles to his rivals Aeschylus and Euripides. He considered *Oedipus the King* the perfect example of tragic form, and developed his theory of tragedy from his analysis of it.

Sophocles' fellow citizens respected him sufficiently to vote him into high city office on at least three occasions. He served for a year as chief tribute-collector for Athens' overseas empire. A controversial claim by Aristophanes of Byzantium, in the third century, implies that Sophocles' tribe was so impressed by a production of *Antigone* that they voted him in as one of ten military generals (*strategoi*) in 441–440. Later in life Sophocles was respected as a participant in democratic governance at the highest level. In 411 he was elected to a ten-man commission charged with replacing Athens' discredited democratic governance with an oligarchy, a development that followed the military's catastrophic defeat in Sicily in 413.

Most ancient biographical sources attest to Sophocles' good looks, his easygoing manner, and his enjoyment of life. Athanaeus' multivolume *Deipnosophistai*, a compendium of gossip and dinner chat about and among ancient worthies, includes several vivid passages that reveal Sophocles as both a commanding presence and an impish prankster, ready one moment to put down a schoolmaster's boorish literary criticism and the next to flirt with the wine boy.

Sophocles is also convincingly described as universally respected, with amorous inclinations and intensely religious qualities that, to his contemporaries, did not seem incompatible. Religious piety meant something quite different to an Athenian than the humility, sobriety, and aversion to sensual pleasure it might suggest to us—officially, if not actually. His involvement in various cults, including one dedicated to a god of health and another to the hero Herakles, contributed to his reputation as "loved by the gods" and "the most religious of men." He was celebrated—and worshipped after his death as a hero—for bringing a healing cult (related to Aesculapius and involving a snake) to Athens. It is possible he founded an early version of a hospital. He never flinched from portraying the Greek gods as often wantonly cruel, destroying innocent people, for instance, as punishment for their ancestors' crimes. But the gods in *Antigone*, *Oedipus at Kolonos*, and *Philoktetes* mete out justice with a more even hand.

One remarkable absence in Sophocles' own life was documented suffering of any kind. His luck continued to the moment his body was placed in its tomb. As he lay dying, a Spartan army had once again invaded the Athenian countryside, blocking access to Sophocles' burial site beyond Athens' walls. But after Sophocles' peaceful death the Spartan general allowed the poet's burial party to pass through his lines, apparently out of respect for the god Dionysos.

Robert Bagg
James Scully

NOTE

1. Unless otherwise indicated, the line numbers and note numbers for translations of Sophocles' dramas other than *Oedipus the King* refer to those in the Harper Perennial *Complete Sophocles* series.

INTRODUCTION
"SOMETHING . . . I REMEMBER . . . WAKES UP TERRIFIED"

The story of a man named Oedipus who unknowingly kills his father and marries his mother goes back at least to Homer.[1] Epic poets and Athenian playwrights in classical times found the story irresistible, and scores tried their hands at it, including Sophocles' contemporaries Aeschylus and Euripides, whose versions survive only in scattered lines or lists of plays produced. Aristotle was fascinated by Sophocles' version. He referred to it often, analyzed its craft astutely, and cited it as the finest example of the playwright's art. Its centrality continues. Because so much of our cultural tradition radiates from it, and because the nerves it touches are so sensitive and its issues so immense, *Oedipus the King* still provokes passionate debate. Is Oedipus, prophesied by Apollo to commit patricide and father children with his mother, truly innocent or in some sense guilty? What does the play imply about the nature of divinity, the family, and the human psyche? If this is the ultimate tragedy, how should we define *tragedy*? Answers to these questions fill many splendid books that discuss the qualities underlying the play's greatness. Such scholarship has been indispensable to me in making this translation, particularly Richard Jebb's and Thomas Gould's translations with commentary.

In Sophocles' time, most Greeks believed the fate of an individual was bound up with a *daimon*, a divinity that presided over every person's life. The Greek word for happiness, *eudaimonia*, meaning "well-daimoned," implies that a person so blessed might be permanently protected. But a *daimon* could quickly and just as often devastate an individual or an entire family. One abiding question *Oedipus the King* asks is whether Oedipus controls his own destiny or whether Apollo and/or a personal divinity, or *daimon*, does.

Sophocles deploys two metaphors to establish his own implicit answer. The first is a common Greek metaphor for a king, general, or statesman—he's a helmsman facing trouble in a storm. This image supports our confidence that a resourceful leader can handle threats from gods or mortals. Oedipus and (initially) all the characters, except the seer Tiresias, view Oedipus as a courageous sailor who can weather problems churned up in his stormy life. But Oedipus' superior intelligence proves of no use in riding out the diabolical dangers he confronts.

The second metaphor appears in a succession of images that show the *daimon* as a dynamic force: it leaps, strikes, or plunges directly at its target. As Oedipus commits each act of violence throughout the play, the *daimon* destroying him would be seen by a Greek audience as present in each blow Oedipus delivers or receives. This audience would also understand that each blow Oedipus struck would, as his life played out, be seen as a blow he struck against himself. Thus Oedipus' consultation with the Delphic oracle, his fatal attack on his father, the sexual mounting of his mother/wife, and his self-blinding near the play's end (when he plunges the pins of Jokasta's brooch into his eyes), as well as the search he undertakes for his true father and for Laios' killer, are all physical aspects of one divine intent: they are blows Apollo struck through Oedipus' own actions that guilefully manipulate Oedipus' proactive nature until it destroys him. Apollo has made Oedipus both his weapon and his victim. Throughout the play, the presence of his *daimon* looms continually in echoes, double meanings, and ironies.

The play opens with Oedipus well established as the king of Thebes. Some fifteen years have passed since Apollo revealed his terrifying prediction to Oedipus, who then refused to return to his home in Korinth. Heading toward Thebes, Oedipus struck and killed a man who attacked him at a three-way intersection, leaving as well the rest of the man's traveling companions for dead. That man, King Laios of Thebes, will prove to be Oedipus' father. When Oedipus, shortly after the violence at the crossroads, risked his life and used his wits to rid Thebes of the Sphinx that tortured the city, grateful Thebans asked him to assume the kingship. He accepted and married Jokasta, Laios' widow, who eventually bore Oedipus' four children.

Now an epidemic has struck Thebes, and the cure requires solving the mystery of Laios' murder. As the investigator, Oedipus naturally refers to himself as the hunter. As he comes closer to discovering his own responsibility, we realize Oedipus is the one being hunted. The audience (who will be familiar with the Oedipus myth) feels the *daimon*'s effect in the first scene, when Oedipus tells his people that though each of them is sick, none is so sick as he, and again when Jokasta's brother Kreon describes

Laios' disappearance: "He told us his journey would take him /
into god's presence. He never came back" (129–130). The word
expanded and translated with the phrase "take him into god's
presence" is *theoros*, which normally refers to a pilgrim or dev-
otee who sees or takes part in a holy event or rite. By using
that word, Kreon implies that Laios' destination was Delphi.
But by not naming Delphi, Sophocles can use the inclusiveness
of the word *theoros* to suggest that "god's presence" might be
manifest in a consultation with Apollo at Delphi or in an out-
of-control encounter on a road.

In the middle of a speech in which Jokasta intends to prove
Oedipus' innocence, she supplies the detail that informs Oedipus of his almost certain guilt. Long ago, a prophecy warned
"that Laios was destined to die / at the hands of a son born
to him and me. / Yet, as rumor had it, foreign bandits / killed
Laios at a place where three roads meet" (829–832). Hearing
those last words strikes Oedipus a physical blow, as Jokasta
instantly notices. (An actor portraying Oedipus should react
to her speech: perhaps start, stare, freeze, or shudder.) Jokasta
asks him about his reaction. He replies, "Just now, something
you said made my heart race. / Something . . . I remember . . .
wakes up terrified" (844–845). He proceeds to tell his wife in
detail how he left Korinth, visited Apollo at Delphi, and killed
a man on his way to Thebes.

The play's spare, ingenious, and suspenseful plot, its bravura
characterizations, unflagging eloquence, and terrifying subject
set it apart. But *how* this artistry intensifies the terror is worth
pursuing. We learn, well into the play, that Apollo's priests at
Delphi communicated an existential threat to Oedipus' parents:

their newborn would kill his father. Jokasta and Laios took an immediate preventive measure by giving the infant to a shepherd with instructions to expose him far from Thebes on the mountain where Laios' flocks grazed. But the shepherd, moved by compassion, disobeyed and gave the infant to a fellow shepherd from Korinth. Clearly Oedipus' parents did not take into account how human kindness might upset their plans—and Apollo was perfectly willing to use such kindness to outwit his victims.

Meanwhile, Oedipus conceptualizes the task of finding Laios' killers: "unless I can mesh some clue I hold / with something known of the killer, I will / be tracking him alone, on a cold trail" (265–267). *Symbolon*, the word translated as "clue," was a physical object, part of a larger whole, typically a jagged potsherd (*ostrakon*) that would fit with another potsherd to authenticate a message brought by a stranger, for instance, or to reunite long-lost kin. By simply using the word *symbolon*, Sophocles invokes the context of a child finding its lost parents. As the action unfolds, Oedipus will "mesh" many clues, but the decisive fit occurs when two men meet onstage after many years: the compassionate Theban herdsman and his friend, the Korinthian shepherd who took Oedipus from him and then saw to it that the child would be raised by King Polybos of Korinth.

This same Korinthian now brings news that seems to prove Apollo's prophecy wrong. Polybos, the 'father' whom Oedipus believed Apollo had predicted he would kill, has died, and Oedipus is his designated heir. But the reunion of the Korinthian and the herdsman, who both admit to their earlier

actions, irretrievably links Oedipus' Korinthian life to his birth
in Thebes as the son of Jokasta and Laios.

The two shepherds are, in the flesh, halves of the *symbolon*
Oedipus believed from the start he must find; their coming together onstage becomes the living symbol whose destructive effect extends beyond prediction or intuition. Now that he has
meshed this last final clue with its other half, Oedipus sees his
killing and incest as parts of a monstrous, divinely ordained
whole—and we see it as a series of events that could not have
happened had not a man taken pity on a child left to die. While
such compassion is never universal, it thrives within a healthy
culture or a loving family. Unforgivable violations of familial
love, in fact, drive the plots of all the Athenian theater's dynas-
tic plays.

Oedipus, who refuses to forgive himself for killing his father and defiling his mother, his children, and himself, sees no
escape from the unbreakable embrace of his family, be it loving
or crushing. This conviction leads Oedipus to one of his finest
and most shocking imaginative leaps. In his misery he names
what creates all families, the sexual act in marriage, and declares *it* the source of humankind's self-immolation: "O marriages! You marriages! You created us, / we sprang to life, then
from the same seed / you burst fathers, brothers, sons, / kinsmen
shedding kinsmen's blood, / brides and mothers and wives—the
most loathsome / atrocities that strike mankind" (1591–1596).

Where the bonds of love are most intense, the danger is
greatest. Oedipus knows he has suffered more of this potential
misery than any other man, but he also immediately declares
that all humankind is equally vulnerable. He realizes that love

itself, which causes such pain, is the irresistible weapon Apollo has used against him. He is the victim of his loyalties—loyalties through which the god controls his responses and his choices.

In his grief, Oedipus foresees a barren and lonely future for his daughters, whom no man will marry because they carry the family's curse. He takes his daughters in his arms as he speaks to them. We see the tangible result of incest here; the father's arms are the brother's. Sophocles focuses our attention on what remains of this family, not on the gods. Oedipus' love is as palpable to us at the end of the play as his wrath, his intelligence, his energy, and his special relation with divinity. This side of his character is uppermost in our minds as we leave the theater. It reminds us of a truth that might be lost in the fury of the drama, that the intensity of his love for his family and his city underlies the intensity of his misery, and is as full, if unwitting, a partner in his destruction as divinity itself.

NOTE

1. *Odyssey* (11. 211ff.), "And I saw the mother of Oedipus, beautiful Epicaste. / What a monstrous thing she did, in all innocence— / she married her own son . . . / who'd killed his own father, then he married *her*! / But the gods soon made it known to all mankind. / So he in growing pain ruled on in beloved Thebes, / lording Cadmus' people— thanks to the gods' brutal plan— / while she went down to Death who guards the massive gates. / Lashing a noose to a steep rafter, there she hanged aloft, / strangling in all her anguish, leaving her son to bear / a world of horrors a mother's Furies bring to life."

Oedipus the King

The play opens in front of the royal palace in Thebes. The palace has an imposing central double door flanked by two altars: one to Apollo, one to household gods. The Delegation of Thebans enters carrying olive branches wound with wool strips. They gather by the palace stairs. The light and atmosphere are oppressive. OEDIPUS enters through the great doors.

OEDIPUS

My children—*you* are the fresh green life
old Kadmos nurtures and protects.
Why do you surge at *me* like this—
with your wool-strung boughs? While
the city is swollen with howls of pain,
reeking incense, and prayers sung
to the Healing God? To have others
tell me these things would not be right,
my sons. So I've come out myself.
My name is Oedipus—the famous—   10
as everyone calls me.

                Tell me, old man,
yours is the natural voice for the rest,
what troubles you? You're terrified?
Looking for reassurance? Be certain
I'll give you all the help I can.
I'd be a hard man if an approach
like yours failed to rouse my pity.

PRIEST

You rule our land, Oedipus! You can see
who comes to your altars, how varied
we are in years: children too weak-winged   20
to fly far, others hunched with age,
a few priests—I am a priest of Zeus—
joined by the best of our young lads.
More of us wait with wool-strung boughs
in the markets, and at Athena's two temples.
Some, at Ismenos' shrine, are watching

ashes for the glow of prophecy.
You can see our city going under,
too feeble to lift its head clear
of the angry murderous waves.   30
Plague blackens our flowering farmland,
sickens our cattle where they graze.
Our women in labor give birth to nothing.
A burning god rakes his fire through our town.
He hates us with fever, he empties
the House of Kadmos, enriching
black Hades with our groans and tears.
We haven't come to beg at your hearth
because we think you're the gods' equal.
We've come because you are the best man   40
at handling trouble or confronting gods.
You came to Thebes, you freed us
from the tax we paid with our lives
to that rasping Singer. You did it with no
help from us. We had nothing to teach you.

People say—they believe!—you had a god's
help when you restored life to our city.
Oedipus, we need *now* the great power
men everywhere know you possess.
Find some way to protect us—learn it   50
from a god's intimation, or a man's.
This much I know: guidance
from men proven right in the past
will meet a crisis with the surest force.
Act as our greatest man! Act

as you did when you first seized fame!
We believe your nerve saved us then.
Don't let us look back on your rule and say,
He lifted us once, but then let us down.
Put us firmly back on our feet,   60
so Thebes will never fall again.

You were a bird from god, you brought good luck
the day you rescued us. Be that man now!
If you want to rule us, it's better
to rule the living than a barren waste.
Walled cities and ships are worthless—
when they've been emptied of people.

OEDIPUS

I do pity you, children. Don't think I'm unaware.
I know what need brings you: this sickness
ravages all of you. Yet, sick as you are,   70
not one of you suffers a sickness like mine.
Yours is a private grief, you feel
only what touches you. But my heart grieves
for you, for myself, and for our city.
You've come to wake me to all this.
There was no need. I haven't been sleeping.
I have wept tears enough, for long enough.
My mind has raced down every twisting path.
And after careful thought, I've set in motion
the only cure I could find: I've sent Kreon,   80
my wife's brother, to Phoibos at Delphi,
to hear what action or what word of mine

will save this town. Already, counting the days,
I'm worried: what is Kreon doing?
He takes too long, more time than he needs.
But when he comes, I'll be the guilty one—
if I don't do all the gods show me to do.

PRIEST

Well timed! The moment you spoke,
your men gave the sign: Kreon's arriving.

OEDIPUS

O Lord Apollo   90
may the luck he brings save us! Luck so bright
we can see it—just as we see him now.

*KREON enters from the countryside, wearing a laurel crown speckled
with red.*

PRIEST

He must bring pleasing news. If not, why would
he wear laurel dense with berries?

OEDIPUS

We'll know very soon. He's within earshot.
Prince! Brother kinsman, son of Menoikeos!
What kind of answer have you brought from god?

KREON

A good one. No matter how dire, if troubles
turn out well, everything will be fine.

OEDIPUS

What did the god say? Nothing you've said   100
so far alarms or reassures me.

KREON

Do you want me to speak in front of these men?
If so, I will. If not, let's go inside.

OEDIPUS

Speak here, to all of us. I suffer
more for them than for my own life.

KREON

Then I'll report what I heard from Apollo.
He made his meaning very clear.
He commands we drive out what corrupts us,
what sickens our city. We now harbor
something incurable. He says: purge it.   110

OEDIPUS

Tell me the source of our trouble.
How do we cleanse ourselves?

KREON

By banishing a man or killing him. It's blood—
kin murder—that brings this storm on our city.

OEDIPUS

Who is the man god wants us to punish?

KREON

As you know, King, our city was ruled once
by Laios, before you came to take the helm.

OEDIPUS

I've heard as much. Though I never saw him.

KREON

Well, Laios was murdered. Now god tells you
plainly: with your own hands punish   120
the very men whose hands killed Laios.

OEDIPUS

Where do I find these men? How do I track
vague footprints from a bygone crime?

KREON

The god said: here, in our own land.
What we look for we can capture.
What we ignore goes free.

OEDIPUS

Was Laios killed at home? Or in the fields?
Or did they murder him on foreign ground?

KREON

He told us his journey would take him
into god's presence. He never came back.   130

OEDIPUS

Did none of his troop see and report
what happened? Isn't there anyone
to question whose answers might help?

KREON

All killed but a single terrified
survivor, able to tell us but one fact.

OEDIPUS

What was it? One fact might lead to many,
if we had one small clue to give us hope.

KREON

They had the bad luck, he said, to meet bandits
who struck them with a force many hands strong.
This wasn't the violence of one man only.   140

OEDIPUS

What bandit would dare commit such a crime . . .
unless somebody here had hired him?

KREON

That was our thought, but after Laios
died, we were mired in new troubles—
and no avenger came.

OEDIPUS

But here was your kingship murdered!
What kind of trouble could have blocked your search?

KREON

The Sphinx's song. So wily, so baffling!
She forced us to forget the dark past,
to confront what lay at our feet.   150

OEDIPUS

Then I'll go back, start fresh,
and light up that darkness.
Apollo was exactly right, and so were you,
to turn our minds back to the murdered man.
It's time I joined your search for vengeance.
Our country and the god deserve no less.

This won't be on behalf of distant kin—
I'll banish this plague for my own sake.
Laios' killer might one day come for me,
exacting vengeance with that same hand.   160
Defending the dead man serves *my* interest.
Rise, children, quick, up from the altar,
pick up those branches that appeal to god.
Someone go call the people of Kadmos—
tell them I'm ready to do anything.
With god's help our good luck
is assured. Without it we're doomed.

Exit OEDIPUS, into the palace.

PRIEST

Stand up, children. He has proclaimed
himself the cure we came to find.

May god Apollo, who sent the oracle,   170
be our savior and end this plague!

The Delegation of Thebans leaves; the CHORUS *enters.*

CHORUS
What will you say to Thebes,
Voice from Zeus? What sweet sounds
convey your will from golden Delphi
to our bright city?
We're at the breaking point,
our minds are wracked with dread.
Our wild cries reach out to you,
Healing God from Delos—
in holy fear we ask: does your will   180
bring a new threat, or has an old doom
come round again as the years wheel by?
Say it, Great Voice,
you who answer us always,
speak as Hope's golden child.

Athena, immortal daughter of Zeus,
your help is the first we ask—
then Artemis, your sister
who guards our land, throned
in the heart of our city.   190
And Apollo, whose arrows
strike from far off! Our three
defenders against death: come now!

Once before, when ruin threatened,
you drove the flames of fever from our city.
Come to us now!

The troubles I suffer are endless.
The plague attacks our troops.
I can think of no weapon
that will keep a man safe.   200
Our rich earth shrivels what it grows.
Women in labor scream, but no
children are born to ease their pain.
One life after another flies—
you see them pass—
like birds driving their strong wings
faster than flash-fire
to the Deathgod's western shore.

Our city dies as its people die
these countless deaths, her children   210
rot in the streets, unmourned,
spreading more death.
Young wives and gray mothers
wash to our altars, their cries
carry from all sides, sobbing
for help, each lost in her pain.
A hymn rings out to the Healer—
an oboe answers,
keening in a courtyard.
Against all this, Goddess,   220

golden child of Zeus,
send us the bright shining
face of courage.

Force that raging killer, the god Ares,
to turn his back and run from our land.
He wields no weapons of war to kill us,
but burning with his fever,
we shout in the hot blast of his charge.
Blow Ares to the vast sea-room
of Amphitritê, banish him   230
under a booming wind
to jagged harbors in the roiling
seas off Thrace. If night
doesn't finish the god's black work,
the day will finish it.
Lightning lurks
in your fiery will,
O Zeus, our Father. Blast it
into the god who kills us.
Apollo, lord of the morning light,   240
draw back your taut, gold-twined
bowstring, fire the sure arrows
that rake our attackers and keep them at bay.

Artemis, bring your radiance
into battle on bright quick feet
down through the morning hills.
I call on the god whose hair

is bound with gold,
the god who gave us our name,
Bakkhos!—the wine-flushed—who answers   250
the maenads' cries, running
beside them! Bakkhos,
come here on fire,
pine-torch flaring.
Face with us the one god
all the gods hate: Ares!

OEDIPUS has entered while the CHORUS was singing.

OEDIPUS
I heard your prayer. It will be answered
if you trust and obey my words:
pull hard with me, bear down on the one cure
that will stop this plague. Help   260
will come, the evils will be gone.
I hereby outlaw the killer
myself, by my own words, though I'm a stranger
both to the crime and to accounts of it.

But unless I can mesh some clue I hold
with something known of the killer, I will
be tracking him alone, on a cold trail.
Since I've come late to your ranks, Thebans,
and the crime is past history,
there are some things that you,   270
the sons of Kadmos, must tell me.

If any one of you knows how Laios,
son of Labdakos, died, he must
tell me all that he knows.
He should not be afraid to name
himself the guilty one: I swear
he'll suffer nothing worse than exile.
Or if you know of someone else—
a foreigner—who struck the blow, speak up.
I will reward you now. I will thank you always.   280
But if you know the killer and don't speak—
out of fear—to shield kin or yourself,
listen to what that silence will cost you.
I order everyone in my land,
where I hold power and sit as king:

don't let that man under your roof,
don't speak with him, no matter who he is.
Don't pray or sacrifice with him,
don't pour purifying water for him.
I say this to all my people: 290
drive him from your houses.
He is our sickness. He poisons us.
This the Pythian god has shown me.
This knowledge makes me an ally—
of both the god and the dead king.
I pray god that the unseen killer,
whoever he is, and whether he killed
alone or had help, be cursed with a life
as evil as he is, a life
of utter human deprivation.   300

I pray this, too: if he's found at my hearth,
inside my house, and I know he's there,
may the curses I aimed at others punish me.
I charge you all—act on my words,
for my sake and the god's, for our dead land
stripped barren of its harvests,
abandoned by its gods.
Even if god had not forced the issue,
this crime should not have gone uncleansed.
You should have looked to it! The dead man   310
was not only noble, he was your king!
But as my luck would have it,
I have his power, his bed—a wife
who shares our seed. And had she borne
the children of us both, she might
have linked us closer still. But Laios
had no luck fathering children, and Fate
itself came down on his head.
These concerns make me fight for Laios
as I would for my own father.   320
I'll stop at nothing to trace his murder
back to the killer's hand.
I act in this for Labdakos and Polydoros,
for Kadmos and Agenor—all our kings.
I warn those who would disobey me:
god make their fields harvest dust,
their women's bodies harvest death.
                                        O you gods,
let them die from the plague that kills
us now, or die from something worse.

As for the rest of you, who are   330
the loyal sons of Kadmos:
may Justice fight with us,
the gods be always at your side.

CHORUS

King, your curse forces me to speak.
None of us is the killer.
And none of us can point to him.
Apollo ordered us to search.
It's up to him to find the killer.

OEDIPUS

So he must. But what man can force
the gods to act against their will?   340

LEADER

May I suggest a second course of action?

OEDIPUS

Don't stop at two. Not if you have more.

LEADER

Tiresias is the man whose power of seeing
shows him most nearly what Apollo sees.
If we put our questions to him, King,
he could give us the clearest answers.

OEDIPUS

But I've seen to this already.
At Kreon's urging I've sent for him—twice now.
I find it strange that he still hasn't come.

LEADER

There were rumors—too faint and old to be much help.   350

OEDIPUS

What were they? I'll examine every word.

LEADER

They say Laios was killed by some travelers.

OEDIPUS

That's something even I have heard.
But the man who did it—no one sees him.

LEADER

If fear has any hold on him
he won't linger in Thebes, not after
he hears threats of the kind you made.

OEDIPUS

If murder didn't scare him, my words won't.

LEADER

There's the man who will convict him:
god's own prophet, led here at last.   360

God gave to him what he gave no one else:
the truth—it's living in his mind.

Enter TIRESIAS, led by a Boy.

OEDIPUS
Tiresias, you are master of the hidden world.
You can read earth and sky. You know
what knowledge to reveal and what to hide.
Though your eyes can't see it,
your mind is well aware of the plague
that afflicts us. Against it, we have no
savior or defense but you, my Lord.
If you haven't heard it from messengers,   370
we now have Apollo's answer: to end
this plague we must root out Laios' killers.
Find them, then kill or banish them.
Help us do this. Don't begrudge us
what you divine from bird cries, show us
everything prophecy has shown you.
Save Thebes! Save yourself ! Save me!
Wipe out what defiles us, keep
the poison of our king's murder
from poisoning the rest of us.   380
We're in your hands. The best use a man
makes of his powers is to help others.

TIRESIAS
The most terrible knowledge is the kind
it pays no wise man to possess.

I knew this, but I forgot it.
I should never have come here.

OEDIPUS

What? You've come, but with no stomach for this?

TIRESIAS

Let me go home. Your life will then
be easier to bear—and so will mine.

OEDIPUS

It's neither lawful nor humane   390
to hold back god's crucial guidance
from the city that raised you.

TIRESIAS

What you've said has made matters worse.
I won't let that happen to me.

OEDIPUS

For god's sake, if you know something,
don't turn your back on us! We're on our knees.

TIRESIAS

You don't understand! If I spoke
of my grief, then it would be yours.

OEDIPUS

What did you say? You know and won't help?
You would betray us all and destroy Thebes?   400

TIRESIAS

I'll cause no grief to you or me. Why ask
futile questions? You'll learn nothing.

OEDIPUS

So the traitor won't answer.
You would enrage a rock.

                        Still won't speak?
Are you so thick-skinned nothing touches you?

TIRESIAS

You blame your rage on *me*? When you
don't see how she embraces you, this fury
you live with? No, so you blame me.

OEDIPUS

Who wouldn't be enraged? Your refusal
to speak dishonors the city.   410

TIRESIAS

It will happen. My silence can't stop it.

OEDIPUS

If it must happen, you should tell me now.

TIRESIAS

I'd rather not. Rage at that, if you like,
with all the savage fury in your heart.

OEDIPUS

That's right. I *am* angry enough to speak
my mind. I think you helped plot the murder.
Did everything but kill him with your own hands.
Had you eyes, though, I would have said
you alone were the killer.

TIRESIAS

That's your truth? Now hear mine: 420
honor the curse your own mouth spoke.
From this day on, don't speak to me
or to your people here. You are the plague.
You poison your own land.

OEDIPUS

So. The appalling charge has been at last
flushed out, into the open. What makes you
think you'll escape?

TIRESIAS

                 I have escaped.
I nurture truth, so truth guards me.

OEDIPUS

Who taught you this *truth*? Not your prophet's trade.

TIRESIAS

You did. By forcing me to speak.   430

OEDIPUS

Speak what? Repeat it so I understand.

TIRESIAS

You missed what I said the first time?
Are you provoking me to make it worse?

OEDIPUS

I heard you. But you made no sense. Try again.

TIRESIAS

You killed the man whose killer you now hunt.

OEDIPUS

The second time is even more outrageous.
You'll wish you'd never said a word.

TIRESIAS

Shall I feed your fury with more words?

OEDIPUS

Use any words you like. They'll be wasted.

TIRESIAS

I say: you have been living unaware   440
in the most hideous intimacy
with your nearest and most loving kin,
immersed in evil that you cannot see.

OEDIPUS

You think you can blithely go on like this?

TIRESIAS

I can, if truth has any strength.

OEDIPUS

Oh, truth has strength, but you have none.
You have blind eyes, blind ears, and a blind brain.

TIRESIAS

And you're a desperate fool—throwing taunts at me
that these men, very soon, will throw at you.

OEDIPUS

You're living in the grip of black   450
unbroken night! You can't harm me
or any man who can see the sunlight.

TIRESIAS

I'm not the one who will bring you down.
Apollo will do that. You're his concern.

OEDIPUS

Did you make up these lies? Or was it Kreon?

TIRESIAS

Kreon isn't your enemy. You are.

OEDIPUS

Wealth and a king's power,
the skill that wins every time—
how much envy, what malice they provoke!
To rob me of power—power I didn't ask for,   460
but which this city thrust into my hands—
my oldest friend here, loyal Kreon, worked
quietly against me, aching to steal my throne.
He hired for the purpose this fortune-teller—
conniving bogus beggar-priest!—a man
who knows what he wants but cannot seize it,
being but a blind groper in his art.
Tell us now, when or where did you ever
prove you had the power of a seer?
Why—when the Sphinx who barked black songs   470
was hounding us—why didn't you speak up
and free the city? Her riddle wasn't the sort
just anyone who happened by could solve:
prophetic skill was needed. But the kind
you learned from birds or gods failed you. It took
Oedipus, the know-nothing, to silence her.
I needed no help from the birds.
I used my wits to find the answer.
I solved it—the same man for whom you plot
disgrace and exile, so you can   480
maneuver close to Kreon's throne.
But your scheme to rid Thebes of its plague
will destroy both you and the man who planned it.
Were you not so frail, I'd make you
suffer exactly what you planned for me.

LEADER

He spoke in anger, Oedipus—but so
did you, if you'll hear what we think.
We don't need angry words. We need insight—
how best to carry out the god's commands.

TIRESIAS

You may be king, but my right   490
to answer makes me your equal.
In this respect, I am as much
my own master as you are.
You do not own my life.
Apollo does. Nor am I
Kreon's man. Hear me out.
Since you have thrown my blindness at me
I will tell you what your eyes don't see:
what evil you are steeped in.
                            You don't see
where you live or who shares your house.   500
Do you know your parents?
                            You are their enemy
in this life and down there with the dead.
And soon their double curse—
your father's and your mother's—
will lash you out of Thebes
on terror-stricken feet.
Your eyes, which now see life,
will then see darkness.
Soon your shriek will burrow
in every cave, bellow   510

from every mountain outcrop on Kithairon,
when what your marriage means strikes home,
when it shows you the house
that took you in. You sailed
a fair wind to a most foul harbor.
Evils you cannot guess
will bring you down to what you are.
To what your children are.
Go on, throw muck at Kreon,
and at the warning spoken through my mouth.   520
No man will ever be
ground into wretchedness as you will be.

OEDIPUS

Should I wait for him to attack me more?
May you be damned. Go. Leave my house
now! Turn your back and go.

TIRESIAS

I'm here only because you sent for me.

OEDIPUS

Had I known you would talk nonsense,
I wouldn't have hurried to bring you here.

TIRESIAS

I seem a fool to you, but the parents
who gave you birth thought I was wise.   530

OEDIPUS

What parents? Hold on. Who was my father?

TIRESIAS

Today you will be born. Into ruin.

OEDIPUS

You've always got a murky riddle in your mouth.

TIRESIAS

Don't you surpass us all at solving riddles?

OEDIPUS

Go ahead, mock what made me great.

TIRESIAS

Your very luck is what destroyed you.

OEDIPUS

If I could save the city, I wouldn't care.

TIRESIAS

Then I'll leave you to that. Boy, guide me out.

OEDIPUS

Yes, let him lead you home. Here, underfoot,
you're in the way. But when you're gone,   540
you'll give us no more grief.

TIRESIAS

I'll go. But first I must finish
what you brought me to do—
your scowl can't frighten me.
The man you have been looking for,
the one your curses threaten, the man
you have condemned for Laios' death:
I say that man is here.

                You think he's an immigrant,
but he will prove himself a Theban native,
though he'll find no joy in that news.   550
A blind man who still has eyes,
a beggar who's now rich, he'll jab
his stick, feeling the road to foreign lands.

OEDIPUS enters the palace.

He'll soon be shown father and brother
to his own children, son and husband
to the mother who bore him—she took
his father's seed and his seed,
and he took his own father's life.
You go inside. Think through
everything I have said.   560
If I have lied, say of me, then—
I have failed as a prophet.

Exit TIRESIAS.

CHORUS

What man provokes
the speaking rock of Delphi?
This crime that sickens speech
is the work of *his* bloody hands.
Now his feet will need to outrace
a storm of wild horses, for
Apollo is running him down,
armed with bolts of fire.   570
He and the Fates close in,
dread gods who never miss.

From snowfields
high on Parnassos
the word blazes out to us all:
track down the man no one can see.
He takes cover in thick brush.
He charges up the mountain
bull-like to its rocks and caves,
going his bleak, hunted way,   580
struggling to escape the doom
Earth spoke from her sacred mouth.
But that doom buzzes low,
never far from his ear.

Fear is what the man who reads birds
makes us feel, fear we can't fight.
We can't accept what he says
but have no power to challenge him.

We thrash in doubt, we can't see
even the present clearly,   590
much less the future.
And we've heard of no feud
embittering the House
of Oedipus in Korinth
against the House of Laios here,
no past trouble and none now,
no proof that would make us blacken
our king's fame as he seeks
to avenge our royal house
for this murder not yet solved.   600

Zeus and Apollo make no mistakes
when they predict what people do.
But there is no way to tell
whether an earthbound prophet sees
more of the future than we can—
though in knowledge and skill
one person may surpass another.
But never, not till I see the charges
proved against him,
will I give credence   610
to a man who blames Oedipus.
All of us saw his brilliance
prevail when the wingèd virgin
Sphinx came at him: he passed the test
that won the people's love.
My heart can't find him guilty.

KREON enters.

KREON

Citizens, I hear that King Oedipus
has made a fearful charge against me.
I'm here to prove it false.
If he thinks anything I've said or done   620
has made this crisis worse, or injured him,
then I have no more wish to live.
This is no minor charge.
It's the most deadly I could suffer,
if my city, my own people—you!—
believe I'm a traitor.

LEADER

He could have spoken in a flash
of ill-considered anger.

KREON

Did he say *I* persuaded the prophet to lie?

LEADER

That's what he said. What he meant wasn't clear.   630

KREON

When he announced my guilt—tell me,
how did his eyes look? Did he seem sane?

LEADER

I can't say. I don't question what my rulers do.
Here he comes, now, out of the palace.

OEDIPUS enters.

OEDIPUS

So? You come here? You have the nerve
to face me in my own house? When you're exposed
as its master's murderer?
Caught trying to steal my kingship?
In god's name, what weakness did you see
in me that led you to plot this?   640
Am I a coward or a fool?
Did you suppose I wouldn't notice
your subtle moves? Or not fight back?
Aren't you attempting something
downright stupid—to win absolute power
without partisans or even friends?
For that you'll need money—and a mob.

KREON

Now you listen to me.
You've had your say, now hear mine.
Don't judge until you've heard me out.   650

OEDIPUS

You speak shrewdly, but I'm a poor learner
from someone I know is my enemy.

KREON

I'll prove you are mistaken to think that.

OEDIPUS

How can you prove you're not a traitor?

KREON

If you think mindless presumption
is a virtue, then you're not thinking straight.

OEDIPUS

If you think attacking a kinsman
will bring you no harm, you must be mad.

KREON

I'll grant that. Now, how have I attacked you?

OEDIPUS

Did you, or did you not, urge me   660
to send for that venerated prophet?

KREON

And I would still give you the same advice.

OEDIPUS

How long ago did King Laios . . .

KREON

Laios? Did what? Why speak of him?

OEDIPUS

. . . die in that murderous attack?

KREON

That was far back in the past.

OEDIPUS

Did this seer practice his craft here then?

KREON

With the same skill and respect he has now.

OEDIPUS

Back then, did he ever mention my name?

KREON

Not in my hearing.   670

OEDIPUS

Didn't you try to hunt down the killer?

KREON

Of course we did. We found out nothing.

OEDIPUS

Why didn't your expert seer accuse me then?

KREON

I don't know. So I'd rather not say.

OEDIPUS

There is one thing you can explain.

KREON

What's that? I'm holding nothing back.

OEDIPUS

Just this. If that seer hadn't conspired with you,
he would never have called me Laios' killer.

KREON

If he said that, *you heard him*, I didn't.
I think you owe me some answers.   680

OEDIPUS

Question me. I have no blood on my hands.

KREON

Did you marry my sister?

OEDIPUS

Do you expect me to deny that?

KREON

You both have equal power in this country?

OEDIPUS

I give her all she asks.

KREON

Do I share power with you both as an equal?

OEDIPUS

You shared our power and betrayed us with it.

KREON

You're wrong. Think it through rationally, as I have.
Who would prefer the anxiety-filled
life of a king to one that lets him sleep at night—   690
if his share of power still equaled a king's?
Nothing in my nature hungers for power—
for me it's enough to enjoy a king's rights,
enough for any prudent man. All I want,
you give me—and it comes with no fear.
To be king would rob my life of its ease.
How could my share of power be more pleasant
than this painless preeminence, this ready
influence I have? I'm not so misguided
that I would crave honors that are burdens.   700
But as things stand, I'm greeted and wished well
on all sides. Those who want something from you
come to me, their best hope of gaining it.
Should I quit this good life for a worse one?
Treason never corrupts a healthy mind.
I have no love for such exploits.
Nor would I join someone who did.
Test me. Go to Delphi yourself.
Find out whether I brought back
the oracle's exact words. If you find   710

I plotted with that omen-reader, seize me
and kill me—not on your authority
alone, but on mine, for I'd vote my own death.
But don't convict me because of a wild thought
you can't prove, one that only you believe.
There's no justice in your reckless confusion
of bad men with good men, traitors with friends.
To cast off a true friend is like suicide—
killing what you love as much as your life.
Time will instruct you in these truths, for time   720
alone is the sure test of a just man—
but you can know a bad man in a day.

LEADER

That's good advice, my lord—
for someone anxious not to fall.
Quick thinkers can stumble.

OEDIPUS

When a conspirator moves
abruptly and in secret against me,
I must outplot him and strike first.
If I pause and do nothing, he
will take charge, and I will have lost.   730

KREON

What do you want? My banishment?

OEDIPUS

No. It's your death I want.

KREON

Then start by defining "betrayal". . .

OEDIPUS

You talk as though you don't believe me.

KREON

How can I if you won't use reason?

OEDIPUS

I reason in my own interest.

KREON

You should reason in mine as well.

OEDIPUS

In a traitor's interest?

KREON

What if you're wrong?

OEDIPUS

I still must rule.   740

KREON

Not when you rule badly.

OEDIPUS

Did you hear him, Thebes!

KREON

Thebes isn't yours alone. It's mine as well!

LEADER

My Lords, stop this. Here's Jokasta
leaving the palace—just in time
to calm you both. With her help, end your feud.

Enter JOKASTA from the palace.

JOKASTA

Wretched men! Why are you out here
so reckless, yelling at each other?
Aren't you ashamed? With Thebes sick and dying
you two fight out some personal grievance?   750
Oedipus. Go inside. Kreon, go home.
Don't make us all miserable over nothing.

KREON

Sister, it's worse than that. Oedipus,
your husband, threatens either to drive me
from my own country or to have me killed.

OEDIPUS

That's right. I caught him plotting to kill me,
Lady. False prophecy was his weapon.

KREON

I ask the gods to sicken and destroy me
if I did anything you charge me with.

JOKASTA

Believe what he says, Oedipus.   760
Accept the oath he just made to the gods.
Do it for my sake too, and for these men.

LEADER

Give in to him, Lord, we beg you.
With all your mind and will.

OEDIPUS

What do you want me to do?

LEADER

Believe him. This man was never a fool.
Now he backs himself up with a great oath.

OEDIPUS

You realize what you're asking?

LEADER

I do.

OEDIPUS

Then say it to me outright.   770

LEADER

Groundless rumor shouldn't be used by you
to scorn a friend who swears his innocence.

OEDIPUS

You know, when you ask this of me
you ask for my exile—or my death.

LEADER

No! We ask neither. By the god
outshining all others, the Sun—
may I die the worst death possible, die
godless and friendless, if I want those things.
This dying land grinds pain into my soul—
grinds it the more if the bitterness   780
you two stir up adds to our misery.

OEDIPUS

Then let him go, though it means my death
or my exile from here in disgrace.
What moves my pity are your words, not his.
He will be hated wherever he goes.

KREON

You are as bitter when you yield
as you are savage in your rage.
But natures like your own
punish themselves the most—
which is the way it should be.   790

OEDIPUS

Leave me alone. Go.

KREON

I'll go. You can see nothing clearly.
But these men see that I'm right.

KREON goes off.

LEADER

Lady, why the delay? Take him inside.

JOKASTA

I will, when you tell me what happened.

LEADER

They had words. One drew a false
conclusion. The other took offense.

JOKASTA

Both sides were at fault?

LEADER

Both sides.

JOKASTA

What did they say?   800

LEADER

Don't ask that. Our land needs no more trouble.
No more trouble! Let it go.

OEDIPUS

I know you mean well when you try to calm me,
but do you realize where it will lead?

LEADER

King, I have said this more than once.
I would be mad, I would lose my good sense,
if I lost faith in you—you
who put our dear country
back on course when you found her
wandering, crazed with suffering.   810
Steer us straight, once again,
with all your inspired luck.

JOKASTA

In god's name, King, tell me, too.
What makes your rage so relentless?

OEDIPUS

I'll tell you, for it's you I respect, not the men.
Kreon brought on my rage by plotting against me.

JOKASTA

Go on. Explain what provoked the quarrel.

OEDIPUS

He says I murdered Laios.

JOKASTA

Does he know this himself? Or did someone tell him?

OEDIPUS

Neither. He sent that crooked seer to make the charge   820
so he could keep his own mouth innocent.

JOKASTA

Then you can clear yourself of all his charges.
Listen to me, for I can make you believe
no man, ever, has mastered prophecy.
This one incident will prove it.
A long time back, an oracle reached Laios—
I don't say Apollo himself sent it,
but the priests who interpret him did.
It said that Laios was destined to die
at the hands of a son born to him and me.   830
Yet, as rumor had it, foreign bandits
killed Laios at a place where three roads meet.

OEDIPUS reacts with sudden intensity to her words.

But the child was barely three days old
when Laios pinned its ankle joints together,
then had it left, by someone else's hands,
high up a mountain far from any roads.
That time Apollo failed to make Laios die
the way he feared—at the hands of his own son.
Doesn't that tell you how much sense

prophetic voices make of our lives?   840
You can forget them. When god wants
something to happen, he makes it happen.
And has no trouble showing what he's done.

OEDIPUS

Just now, something you said made my heart race.
Something . . . I remember . . . wakes up terrified.

JOKASTA

What fear made you turn toward me and say that?

OEDIPUS

I thought you said Laios was struck down
where three roads meet.

JOKASTA

That's the story they told. It hasn't changed.

OEDIPUS

Tell me, where did it happen?   850

JOKASTA

In a place called Phokis, at the junction
where roads come in from Delphi and from Daulis.

OEDIPUS

How long ago was it? When it happened?

JOKASTA

We heard the news just before you came to power.

OEDIPUS

O Zeus! What did you will me to do?

JOKASTA

Oedipus, you look heartsick. What is it?

OEDIPUS

Don't ask me yet. Describe Laios to me.
Was he a young man, almost in his prime?

JOKASTA

He was tall, with some gray salting his hair.
He looked then not very different from you now.   860

OEDIPUS

Like me? I'm finished! It was aimed at me,
that savage curse I hurled in ignorance.

JOKASTA

What did you say, my Lord? Your face scares me.

OEDIPUS

I'm desperately afraid the prophet sees.
Tell me one more thing. Then I'll be sure.

JOKASTA

I'm so frightened I can hardly answer.

OEDIPUS

Did Laios go with just a few armed men,
or the large troop one expects of a prince?

JOKASTA

There were five only, one was a herald.
And there was a wagon, to carry Laios.   870

OEDIPUS

Ah! I see it now. Who told you this, Lady?

JOKASTA

Our slave. The one man who survived and came home.

OEDIPUS

Is he by chance on call here, in our house?

JOKASTA

No. When he returned and saw
that you had all dead Laios' power,
he touched my hand and begged me to send him
out to our farmlands and sheepfolds,
so he'd be far away and out of sight.
I sent him. He was deserving—though a slave—
of a much larger favor than he asked.   880

OEDIPUS

Can you send for him right away?

JOKASTA

Of course. But why do you need him?

OEDIPUS

I'm afraid, Lady, I've said too much.
That's why I want to see him now.

JOKASTA

I'll have him come. But don't I have the right
to know what so deeply disturbs you, Lord?

OEDIPUS

So much of what I dreaded has come true.
I'll tell you everything I fear.
No one has more right than you do
to know the risks to which I'm now exposed.   890
Polybos of Korinth was my father.
My mother was Merope, a Dorian.
I was the leading citizen, when Chance
struck me a sudden blow.
Alarming as it was, I took it
much too hard. At a banquet,
a man who had drunk too much wine
claimed I was not my father's son.
Seething, I said nothing. All that day
I barely held it in. But next morning   900
I questioned Mother and Father. Furious,
they took their anger out on the man
who shot the insult. They reassured me.
But the rumor still rankled; it hounded me.

So with no word to my parents,
I traveled to the Pythian oracle.
But the god would not honor me
with the knowledge I craved.

                    Instead,
his words flashed other things—
horrible, wretched things—at me: 910
I would be my mother's lover.
I would show the world children
no one could bear to look at. I
would murder the father whose seed I am.
When I heard that, and ever after,
I traced the road back to Korinth
only by looking at the stars. I fled
to somewhere I'd never see outrages,
like those the god promised, happen to me.
But my flight carried me to just the place   920
where, you tell me, the king was killed.
Oh, woman, here is the truth. As I approached
the place where three roads joined,
a herald, a colt-drawn wagon, and a man
like the one you describe, met me head-on.
The man out front and the old man himself
began to crowd me off the road.
The driver, who's forcing me aside,
I smash in anger.

               The old man watches me,
he measures my approach, then leans out   930
lunging with his two-spiked goad
dead at my skull. He's more than repaid:

I hit him so fast with the staff
this hand holds, he's knocked back
rolling off the cart. Where he lies, face up.
And then I kill them all.

But if this stranger and Laios . . . were the same blood,
whose triumph could be worse than mine?
Is there a man alive the gods hate more?
Nobody, no Theban, no foreigner,   940
can take me to his home.
No one can speak with me.
They all must drive me out.
I am the man—no one else—
who laid this curse on myself.
I make love to his wife with hands
repulsive from her husband's blood.
Can't you see that I'm evil?
My whole nature, utter filth?
Look, I must be banished. I must   950
never set eyes on my people, never
set foot in my homeland, because . . .
I'll marry my own mother,
kill Polybos, my father,
who brought me up and gave me birth.
If someone said things like these
must be the work of a savage god,
he'd be speaking the truth. O you
pure and majestic gods! Never,
never, let the day such things happen   960
arrive for me. Let me never see it.

Let me vanish from men's eyes
before that doom comes down on me.

OEDIPUS THE KING *(Gk 831-847)*

JOKASTA

What you say terrifies us, Lord. But don't lose hope
until you hear from the eyewitness.

OEDIPUS

That is the one hope I have left—to wait
for this man to come in from the fields.

JOKASTA

When he comes, what do you hope to hear?

OEDIPUS

This: if his story matches yours,
I will have escaped disaster.   970

JOKASTA

What did I say that would make such a difference?

OEDIPUS

He told you Laios was killed by bandits.
If he still claims there were several,
then I cannot be the killer. One man
cannot be many. But if he says: one man,
braving the road alone, did it,
there's no more doubt.
The evidence will drag me down.

JOKASTA

You can be sure that was the way
he first told it. How can he take it back?   980
The entire city heard him, not just me.
Even if now he changes his story,
Lord, he could never prove that Laios'
murder happened as the god predicted.

                                  Apollo
said plainly: my son would kill Laios.
That poor doomed child had no chance
to kill his father, for he was killed first.
After that, no oracle ever
made me look right, then left, in fear.

OEDIPUS

You've thought this out well. Still, you must   990
send for that herdsman. Don't neglect this.

JOKASTA

I'll send for him now. But come inside.
Would I do anything to displease you?

OEDIPUS and JOKASTA enter the palace.

CHORUS

Let it be my good luck
to win praise all my life
for respecting the sky-walking laws,
born to stride

through the light-filled heavens.
Olympos
alone was their father.   1000
No human mind could conceive them.
Those laws
neither sleep nor forget—
a mighty god lives on in them
who does not age.

A violent will
fathers the tyrant,
and violence, drunk
on wealth and power,
does him no good.   1010
He scales the heights—
until he's thrown
down to his doom,
where quick feet are no use.
But there's another fighting spirit
I ask god never to destroy—
the kind that makes our city thrive.
That god will protect us
I will never cease to believe.

But if a man   1020
speaks and acts with contempt—
flouts the law, sneers
at the stone gods in their shrines—
let a harsh death punish

his doomed indulgence.
Even as he wins he cheats—
he denies himself nothing—
his hand reaches for things
too sacred to be touched.
When crimes like these, which god hates,   1030
are not punished—but *honored*—
what good man will think his own life
safe from god's arrows piercing his soul?
Why should I dance to *this* holy song?

Here the CHORUS stops dancing and speaks the next strophe motionless.

If prophecies don't show the way
to events all men can see,
I will no longer honor
the holy place untouchable:
Earth's navel at Delphi.
I will not go to Olympia   1040
nor the temple at Abai.
You, Zeus who hold power, if Zeus
lord of all is really who you are,
look at what's happening here:
prophecies made to Laios fade;
men ignore them;
Apollo is nowhere
glorified with praise.
The gods lose force.

JOKASTA enters from the palace carrying a suppliant's branch and some
smoldering incense. She approaches the altar of Apollo near the palace
door.

JOKASTA

Lords of my country, this thought   1050
came to me: to visit the gods' shrines
with incense and a bough in my hands.
Oedipus lets alarms of every kind
inflame his mind. He won't let past
experience calm his present fears,
as a man of sense would.
He's at the mercy of everybody's
terrifying words. Since he won't listen to me,
Apollo—you're the nearest god—

Enter MESSENGER from the countryside.

I come praying for your good will. Look,   1060
here is my branch. Cleanse us, cure our sickness.
When we see Oedipus distraught, we all shake,
as though sailing with a fearful helmsman.

MESSENGER

Can you point out to me, strangers,
the house where King Oedipus lives? Better
yet, tell me if you know where he is now.

LEADER

That's the house where he lives, stranger. He's inside.
This woman is his wife and mother . . . of his children.

MESSENGER

I wish her joy, and the family joy
that comes when a marriage bears fruit.   1070

JOKASTA

And joy to you, stranger, for those kind words.
What have you to tell us? Or to ask?

MESSENGER

Great news, Lady, for you and your mate.

JOKASTA

What news? Who sent you to us?

MESSENGER

I come from Korinth.
You'll rejoice at my news, I'm sure—
but it may also make you grieve.

JOKASTA

What? How can it possibly do both?

MESSENGER

They're going to make him king. So say
the people who live on the isthmus.   1080

JOKASTA

Isn't old Polybos still in power?

MESSENGER

No longer. Death has laid him in the tomb.

JOKASTA

You're saying, old man, Polybos has died?

MESSENGER

Kill me if that's not the truth.

JOKASTA speaks to a maid, who then runs inside.

JOKASTA

Girl, run to your master with the news.
You oracles of the gods! Where are you now?
The man Oedipus feared he would kill,
the man he ran from, that man's dead.
Chance killed him. Not Oedipus. Chance!

OEDIPUS enters quickly from the palace.

OEDIPUS

Darling Jokasta, my loving wife,   1090
why did you ask me to come out?

JOKASTA

Listen to what this man has to say.
See what it does to god's proud oracle.

OEDIPUS

Where's he from? What's his news?

JOKASTA

From Korinth. Your father isn't . . .
Polybos . . . is no more . . . he's dead.

OEDIPUS

Say it, old man. I want to hear it from your mouth.

MESSENGER

If plain fact is what you want first,
have no doubt he is dead and gone.

OEDIPUS

Was it treason, or did disease bring him down?   1100

MESSENGER

A slight push tips an old man into stillness.

OEDIPUS

Then some sickness killed him?

MESSENGER

That, and the long years he had lived.

OEDIPUS

Oh, yes, wife! Why should we scour Pythian smoke
or fear birds shrieking overhead?

If signs like these had been telling the truth,
I would have killed my father. But he's dead.
He's safely in the ground. And here I am,
who didn't lift a spear. Or did he
die of longing for me? That might   1110
have been what my killing him meant.
Polybos' death has dragged all those
worthless oracles with him to Hades.

JOKASTA

Didn't I tell you that before?

OEDIPUS

You did. But I was still driven by fear.

JOKASTA

Don't let these things worry you anymore.

OEDIPUS

Not worry that I'll share my mother's bed?

JOKASTA

Why should a human being live in fear?
Chance rules our lives!
Who has any sure knowledge of the future?   1120
It's best to take life as it comes.
This marriage with your mother—don't fear it.
In their dreams, before now, many men
have slept with their mothers.

Those who believe such things mean nothing
will have an easier time in life.

OEDIPUS

A brave speech! I would like to believe it.
But how can I if my mother's still living?
While she lives, I will live in fear,
no matter how persuasive you are.   1130

JOKASTA

Your father's tomb shines a great light.

OEDIPUS

On him, yes! But I fear her. She's alive.

MESSENGER

What woman do you fear?

OEDIPUS

I dread that oracle from the god, stranger.

MESSENGER

Would it be wrong for someone else to know it?

OEDIPUS

No, you may hear it. Apollo told me
I would become my mother's lover, that I
would have my father's blood on these hands.
Because of that, I haven't gone near Korinth.

So far, I've been very lucky—and yet,   1140
there's no greater pleasure than to
look our own parents in the eyes!

MESSENGER

Did this oracle drive you into exile?

OEDIPUS

I didn't want to kill my father, old man.

MESSENGER

Then why haven't I put your fears to rest,
King? I came here hoping to be useful.

OEDIPUS

I would give anything to be free of fear.

MESSENGER

I confess I came partly for that reason—
to be rewarded when you've come back home.

OEDIPUS

I will never live where my parents live.   1150

MESSENGER

My son, you can't possibly know what you're doing.

OEDIPUS

Why is that, old man? In god's name, tell me.

MESSENGER

Is it because of them you won't go home?

OEDIPUS

I am afraid Apollo spoke the truth.

MESSENGER

Afraid you'd do your parents unforgivable harm?

OEDIPUS

Exactly that, old man. I am in constant fear.

MESSENGER

Your fear is groundless. Do you understand?

OEDIPUS

How can it be groundless if I'm their son?

MESSENGER

But Polybos was no relation to you.

OEDIPUS

What? Polybos was not my father?   1160

MESSENGER

No more than I am. Exactly the same.

OEDIPUS

How the same? He fathered me and you didn't.

MESSENGER

He didn't father you any more than I did.

OEDIPUS

Why did he say, then, that I was his son?

MESSENGER

He took you from my hands as a gift.

OEDIPUS

He loved me so much—knowing I came from you?

MESSENGER

He had no children of his own to love.

OEDIPUS

And you? Did you buy me? Or find me somewhere?

MESSENGER

I found you in the wooded hollows of Kithairon.

OEDIPUS

Why were you wandering way out there?   1170

MESSENGER

I had charge of the sheep grazing those slopes.

OEDIPUS

A migrant hired to work our flocks?

MESSENGER

I saved your life that day, my son.

OEDIPUS

When you picked me up, what was wrong with me?

MESSENGER

Your ankles know. Let them tell you.

OEDIPUS

Ahh! Why do you bring up that ancient wound?

MESSENGER

Your ankles had been pinned. I set you free.

OEDIPUS

From birth I've carried the shame of those scars.

MESSENGER

That was the luck that named you, Oedipus.

OEDIPUS

Did my mother or my father do this to me?　　　　1180
Speak the truth for god's sake.

MESSENGER

I don't know. The man who gave you to me
will know.

OEDIPUS

>You took me from someone?
You didn't chance on me yourself?

MESSENGER

I took you from another shepherd.

OEDIPUS

Who was he? Tell me plainly as you can.

MESSENGER

He was known as someone who worked for Laios.

OEDIPUS

The same Laios who was once king *here*?

MESSENGER

The same. This man worked as his shepherd.

OEDIPUS

Is he alive? Can I see him?   1190

MESSENGER

Someone from here could answer that better.

OEDIPUS

Does anyone here know what has become
of this shepherd? Has anyone seen him
in town or in the fields? Speak up now.
The time has come to make everything known.

LEADER

I believe he means that same herdsman
you've already sent for. Your wife
would be the best one to ask.

OEDIPUS

                                        Lady, do you
recall the man we sent for?
Is that the man he means?   1200

JOKASTA

Why ask about him? Don't listen to him.
Ignore his words. Forget he said them.

OEDIPUS

With clues like these in my hands, how can I
fail to solve the mystery of my birth?

JOKASTA

For god's sake, if you care about your life,
give up your search. Let my pain be enough!

OEDIPUS

You'll be fine! What if my mother was born
from slaves—from three generations of slaves—
how could that make you lowborn?

JOKASTA

Listen to me: I beg you. Don't do this.   1210

OEDIPUS

I cannot listen. I must have the truth.

JOKASTA

I'm thinking only of what's best for you.

OEDIPUS

What's best for me exasperates me now.

JOKASTA

You poor child! Never find out who you are.

OEDIPUS

Someone, bring me the herdsman. Let
that woman glory in her precious birth.

JOKASTA

Oh you poor doomed child! That is the only name
I can call you now. None other, forever!

JOKASTA runs into the palace.

LEADER

Why has she left like that, Oedipus,
driven off by a savage grief? I'm afraid   1220
something horrendous will break this silence.

OEDIPUS

Let it burst! My seed may well *be* common!
Even so, I still must know who I am.

The meanness of my birth may shame
her womanly pride. But since, in my
own eyes, I am the child of Luck—
she is the source of my well-being—
never will I be dishonored.
Luck is the mother who raised me. The months
are my brothers, who've seen me through   1230
the low times in my life and the high ones.
Those are the powers that made me.
I could never betray them *now*—
by calling off the search
for the secret of my birth!

CHORUS
By the gods of Olympos, if I have
a prophet's range of eye and mind—
tomorrow's moonlight
will shine on you, Kithairon.
Oedipus will honor you—   1240
his native mountain,
his nurse, his mother. Nothing
will keep us from dancing
then, mountain joyful to our king!
We call out to Phoibos Apollo:
be the cause of our joy!

CHORUS *turns toward OEDIPUS.*

My son, who was your mother?
Which nymph bore you to Pan,

the mountain rover?
Was it Apollo's bride   1250
to whom you were born
in the grassy highlands?
Or did Hermes, Lord of Kyllene,
or Bakkhos of the mountain peaks,
take you—a sudden joy—
from nymphs of Helikon,
whose games he often shares?

OEDIPUS

Old men, if it's possible
to recognize a man I've never met,
I think I see the herdsman we've been waiting for.   1260
Our fellow would be old, like the stranger approaching.
Those leading him are my own men.
But I expect you'll know him better.
Some of you will know him by sight.

Enter HERDSMAN, led by OEDIPUS' Attendants.

LEADER

I do know him. He is from Laios' house,
a trustworthy shepherd if he ever had one.

OEDIPUS

Korinthian, I'll ask you to speak first:
is this the man you mean?

MESSENGER

You're looking at him.

OEDIPUS

Now you, old man. Look at me.   1270

Answer every question I ask you.

Did you once come from Laios' house?

HERDSMAN

I did. I wasn't a bought slave.

I was born and raised in their house.

OEDIPUS

What was your job? How did you spend your time?

HERDSMAN

My life I have spent tending sheep.

OEDIPUS

In what region did you normally work?

HERDSMAN

Mainly Kithairon, and the country thereabouts.

OEDIPUS gestures toward the MESSENGER.

OEDIPUS

That man. Do you recall ever seeing him?

HERDSMAN

Recall how? Doing what? Which man?   1280

OEDIPUS goes to the MESSENGER and puts his hand on him.

OEDIPUS

This man right here. Have you ever seen him before?

HERDSMAN

Not that I recognize—not right away.

MESSENGER

It's no wonder, master. His memory's faded,
but I'll revive it for him. I'm sure he knows me.
We worked the pastures on Kithairon together—
he with his two flocks, me with one—
for three whole grazing seasons, from early spring
until Arcturos rose. When the weather turned cold
I'd drive my sheep home to their winter pens.
He'd drive his away to Laios' sheepfolds.   1290
Do I describe what happened, old friend? Or don't I?

HERDSMAN

That's the truth, but it was so long ago.

MESSENGER

Do you remember giving me a boy
I was to raise as my own son?

HERDSMAN

What? Why ask me that?

MESSENGER

There, my friend, is the man who was that boy.

The MESSENGER nods toward OEDIPUS.

HERDSMAN

Damn you! Shut up and say nothing.

OEDIPUS

Don't attack him for speaking, old man.
Your words beg to be punished more than his.

HERDSMAN

Tell me, royal master, what've I done wrong?   1300

OEDIPUS

You didn't answer him about the boy.

HERDSMAN

He's trying to make something out of nothing.

OEDIPUS

Speak of your own free will. Or under torture.

HERDSMAN

Dear god! I'm an old man. Don't hurt me.

OEDIPUS

One of you, bind his arms behind his back.

Attendants approach the HERDSMAN *and start to seize his arms.*

HERDSMAN

Why this, you doomed man? What else must you know?

OEDIPUS

Did you give him the child, as he claims you did?

HERDSMAN

I did. I wish that day I had died.

OEDIPUS

You will die if you don't speak the truth.

HERDSMAN

Answering you is what will get me killed.   1310

OEDIPUS

I think this man is deliberately stalling.

HERDSMAN

No! I've said it once. I gave him the boy.

OEDIPUS

Was the boy from your house? Or someone else's?

HERDSMAN

Not from my house. Someone gave him to me.

OEDIPUS

The person! Name him! From what house?

HERDSMAN

Don't ask me that, master. For god's sake, don't.

OEDIPUS

If I have to ask one more time, you'll die.

HERDSMAN

He was a child from the house of Laios.

OEDIPUS

A slave? Or a child born of Laios' blood?

HERDSMAN

Help me! I am about to speak terrible words.   1320

OEDIPUS

And I to hear them. But hear them I must!

HERDSMAN

The child was said to be Laios' own son.
Your lady in the house would know that best.

OEDIPUS

She gave the child to you?

HERDSMAN

She gave him, King.

OEDIPUS

To do what?

HERDSMAN

I was to let it die.

OEDIPUS

Kill her own child?

HERDSMAN

She feared prophecies.

OEDIPUS

What prophecies?

HERDSMAN

That this child would kill his father.

OEDIPUS

Why, then, did you give him to this old man?

HERDSMAN

Out of pity, master. I hoped this man   1330
would take him back to his own land.
But that man saved him for this—
the worst grief of all. If the child
he speaks of is you, master, now you
know: your birth has doomed you.

OEDIPUS

All! All! It has all happened!
It was all true. O light! Let this
be the last time I look on you.
You see now who I am—
the child who must not be born!   1340
I loved where I must not love!
I killed where I must not kill!

OEDIPUS runs into the palace.

CHORUS

Men and women who live and die,
I set no value on your lives.
Which one of you ever, reaching
for blessedness that lasts,
finds more than what *seems* blest?
You live in that seeming
a while, then it vanishes.
Your fate teaches me this, Oedipus,   1350
yours, you suffering man, the story

god spoke through you: never
call any man fortunate.

O Zeus, no man drew a bow like this man!
He shot his arrow home,
winning power, pleasure, wealth.
He killed the virgin Sphinx,
who sang the god's dark oracles;
her claws were hooked and sharp.
He fought off death in our land;   1360
he towered against its threat.
Since those times I've called you my king,
honoring you mightily, my Oedipus,
who wielded the great might of Thebes.

But now—nobody's story
has the sorrow of yours.
O my so famous Oedipus—
the same great harbor
welcomed you
first as child, then as father   1370
tumbling upon your bridal bed.
How could the furrows your father plowed, doomed
man, how could they suffer so long in silence?

Time, who sees all, caught you
living a life you never willed.
Time damns this marriage that is
no marriage, where the fathered child

fathered children himself.
O son of Laios, I wish
I'd never seen you! I fill my lungs,   1380
I sing with all my power
the plain truth in my heart.
Once you gave me new breath,
O my Oedipus!—but now
you close my eyes in darkness.

Enter SERVANT from the palace.

SERVANT

You've always been our land's most honored men.
If you still have a born Theban's love
for the House of Labdakos, you'll be crushed
by what you're about to see and hear.
No rivers could wash this house clean—   1390
not the Danube, not the Rion—
it hides so much evil that now
is coming to light. What happened here
was not involuntary evil. It was willed.
The griefs that punish us the most
are those we've chosen for ourselves.

LEADER

We already knew more than enough
to make us grieve. Do you have more to tell?

SERVANT

It is the briefest news to say or hear.

Our royal lady Jokasta is dead.   1400

LEADER

That pitiable woman. How did she die?

SERVANT

She killed herself. You will be spared the worst—

since you weren't there to see it.

But you will hear, exactly as I can

recall it, what that wretched woman suffered.

She came raging through the courtyard

straight for her marriage bed, the fists

of both her hands clenched in her hair.

Once in, she slammed the doors shut and called out

to Laios, so long dead. She remembered   1410

his living sperm of long ago, who killed Laios,

while she lived on to breed with her son

more ruined children.

                            She grieved for the bed

she had loved in, giving birth

to all those doubled lives—

husband fathered by husband,

children sired by her child.

From this point on I don't know how she died—

Oedipus burst in shouting,

distracting us from her misery.   1420

We looked on, stunned, as he plowed through us,

raging, asking us for a spear,
asking for the wife who was no wife
but the same furrowed twice-mothering Earth
from whom he and his children sprang.
He was frantic, yet some god's hand
drove him toward his wife—none of us near him did.
As though someone were guiding him, he lunged,
with a savage yell, at the double doors,
wrenching the bolts from their sockets.   1430
He burst into the room. We saw her there:
the woman above us, hanging by the neck,
swaying there in a noose of tangled cords.
He saw. And bellowing in anguish
he reached up, loosening the noose that held her.
With the poor lifeless woman laid out on the ground
this, then, was the terror we saw: he pulled
the long pins of hammered gold clasping her gown,
held them up, and punched them into his eyes,
back through the sockets. He was screaming: 1440
"Eyes, now you will not, no, never
see the evil I suffered, the evil I caused.
You will see blackness—where once
were lives you should never have lived to see,
yearned-for faces you so long failed to know."
While he howled out these tortured words—
not once, but many times—his raised hands
kept beating his eyes. The blood kept coming,
drenching his beard and cheeks. Not a few wet drops,
but a black storm of bloody hail lashing his face.   1450

What this man and this woman did
broke so much evil loose! That evil joins
the whole of both their lives in grief.
The happiness they once knew was real,
but now that happiness is in ruins—
wailing, death, disgrace. Whatever misery
we have a name for, is here.

LEADER

Has his grief eased at all?

SERVANT

He shouts for someone to open the door bolts:

"Show this city its father-killer," he cries,   1460
"Show it its mother . . ." He said the word. I can't.
He wants to banish himself from the land,
not doom this house any longer
by living here, under his own curse.
He's so weak, though, he needs to be helped.
No one could stand up under a sickness like his.
Look! The door bolts are sliding open.
You will witness a vision of such suffering
even those it revolts will pity.

OEDIPUS emerges from the slowly opening palace doors. He is blinded, with blood on his face and clothes, but the effect should arouse more awe and pity than shock. He moves with the aid of an Attendant.

LEADER

Your pain is terrible to see,   1470
pure, helpless anguish,
more moving than anything
my eyes have ever touched.
                                        O man of pain,
where did your madness come from?
What god would go
to such inhuman lengths
to savage your defenseless life?
(moans)
I cannot look at you—
though there's so much
to ask you, so much to learn,   1480
so much that holds my eyes—
so strong are the shivers of awe
you send through me.

OEDIPUS

Ahhh! My life
screams in pain.
Where is my misery
taking me?
How far does my voice fly,
fluttering out there
on the wind?   1490
O god, how far have you thrown me?

LEADER

To a hard place. Hard to watch, hard to hear.

OEDIPUS

Darkness buries me in her hate, takes me
in her black hold.
Unspeakable blackness.
It can't be fought off,
it keeps coming,
wafting evil all over me.
Ahhh!
Those goads piercing my eyes,   1500
those crimes stabbing my mind,
strike through me—one deep wound.

LEADER

It is no wonder you feel
nothing but pain now,
both in your mind and in your flesh.

OEDIPUS

Ah, friend, you're still here,
faithful to the blind man.
I know you are near me. Even
in my darkness I know your voice.

LEADER

You terrify us. How could you   1510
put out your eyes? What god drove you to it?

OEDIPUS

It was Apollo who did this.
He made evil, consummate evil,
out of my life.
But the hand
that struck these eyes
was my hand.
I in my wretchedness
struck me, no one else did.
What good was left for my eyes to see?   1520
Nothing in this world could I see now
with a glad heart.

LEADER

That is so.

OEDIPUS

Whom could I look at? Or love?
Whose greeting could I answer
with fondness, friends?
Take me quickly from this place.
I am the most ruined, the most cursed,
the most god-hated man who ever lived.

LEADER

You're broken by what happened, broken   1530
by what's happening in your own mind.
I wish I had never even known you.

OEDIPUS

May he die, the man
who found me in the pasture,
who unshackled my feet,
who saved me from that death for a worse life,
a life I cannot thank him for.
Had I died then, I would have caused
no great grief to my people and myself.

LEADER

I wish he had let you die.   1540

OEDIPUS

I wouldn't have come home to kill my father,
no one could call me lover
of her from whose body I came.
I have no god now.
I'm son to a fouled mother.
I fathered children in the bed
where my father once gave me
deadly life. If ever an evil
rules all other evils
it is my evil, the life   1550
god gave to Oedipus.

LEADER

I wish I could say you acted wisely.
You would have been better off dead than blind.

OEDIPUS

There was no better way than mine.
No more advice! If I had eyes, how could
they bear to look at my father in Hades?
Or at my devastated mother? Not even
hanging could right the wrongs I did them both.
You think I'd find the sight of my children
delightful, born to the life they must live?   1560
Never, ever, delightful to my eyes!
Nor this town, its wall, gates, and towers—
nor sacred images of our gods.
I severed myself from these joys when I
banished the vile killer—myself!—
totally wretched now, though I was raised
more splendidly than any Theban.
But now the gods have proven me
defiled, and of Laios' own blood.
And once I've brought such disgrace on myself,   1570
how could I look calmly on my people?
I could not! If I could deafen my ears
I would. I'd deaden my whole body,
go blind and deaf to shut those evils out.
The silence in my mind would be sweet.
O Kithairon, why did you take me in?
Or once you had seized me, why didn't you
kill me then, leaving no trace of my birth?
O Polybos and Korinth, and that palace
they called the ancient home of my fathers!   1580
I was their glorious boy growing up,
but under that fair skin

festered a hideous disease.
My vile self now shows its vile birth.

                       You,
three roads, and you, darkest ravine,
you, grove of oaks, you, narrow place
where three paths drank blood from my hands,
my fathering blood pouring into you:
Do you remember what I did while you watched?
And when I came here, what I did then?   1590
O marriages! You marriages! You created us,
we sprang to life, then from that same seed
you burst fathers, brothers, sons,
kinsmen shedding kinsmen's blood,
brides and mothers and wives—the most loathsome
atrocities that strike mankind.
I must not name what should not be.
If you love the gods, hide me out there,
kill me, heave me into the sea,
anywhere you can't see me.   1600
Come, take me. Don't shy away. Touch
this human derelict. Don't fear me, trust me.
No other man, only myself,
can be afflicted with my sorrows.

LEADER
Here's Kreon. He's come when you need him,
to take action or to give you advice.
He is the only ruler we have left
to guard Thebes in your place.

OEDIPUS

Can I say anything he'll listen to?
Why would he believe me?   1610
I wronged him so deeply.
I proved myself so false to him.

KREON enters.

KREON

I haven't come to mock you, Oedipus.
I won't dwell on the wrongs you did me.

KREON speaks to the Attendants.

Men, even if you've no respect
for a fellow human being, show some
for the life-giving flame of the Sun god:
don't leave this stark defilement out here.
The Earth, the holy rain, the light, can't bear it.

Quickly, take him back to the palace.   1620
If these sorrows are shared
only among the family,
that will spare us further impiety.

OEDIPUS

Thank god! I feared much worse from you.
Since you've shown me, a most vile man,
such noble kindness, I have one request.
For your sake, not for mine.

KREON

What is it? Why do you ask me like that?

OEDIPUS

Expel me quickly to some place
where no living person will find me.   1630

KREON

I would surely have done that. But first
I need to know what the god wants me to do.

OEDIPUS

He's given his command already.
I killed my father. I am unholy. I must die.

KREON

So the god said. But given
the crisis we're in, we had better
be absolutely sure before we act.

OEDIPUS

You'd ask about a broken man like me?

KREON

Surely, by now, you're willing to trust god.

OEDIPUS

I am. But now I must ask for something   1640
within your power. I beg you! Bury her—
she's lying inside—as you think proper.

Give her the rites due your kinswoman.
As for me, don't condemn my father's city
to house me while I'm still alive.
Let me live out my life on Kithairon,
the very mountain—
the one I've made famous—
that my father and mother chose for my tomb.
Let me die there, as my parents ordained.   1650
And yet, I know this much:
no sickness can kill me. Nothing can.
I was saved from that death
to face an extraordinary evil.
Let my fate take me now, where it will.

My children, Kreon. My sons.
They're grown now. They won't need your help.

They'll find a way to live anywhere.
But my poor wretched girls, who never
ate anywhere but at my table,   1660
they've never lived apart from me.
I fed them with my own hands.
                              Care for them.
If you're willing, let me touch them now,
let me give in to my grief.
Grant it, Kreon, from your great heart.
If I could touch them, I would
imagine them as my eyes once saw them.

*The gentle sobbing of OEDIPUS' two daughters is heard offstage. Soon two
small girls enter.*

What's this?
O gods, are these my children sobbing?
Has Kreon pitied me?   1670
Given me my own dear children?
Has he?

KREON

I have. I brought them to you
because I knew how much joy,
as always, you would take in them.

OEDIPUS

Bless this kindness of yours. Bless your luck.
May the gods guard you better than they did me.
Children, where are you? Come to me.
These are your brother's hands, hands
of the man who created you, hands that caused   1680
my once bright eyes to go dark.
He, children, saw nothing, knew nothing.
He fathered you where his own life began,
where his own seed grew. Though I can't
see you, I can weep for you . . .

—OEDIPUS takes his daughters in his arms—

when I think how bitter your lives will be.
I know the life that men will make you live.
What public gatherings, what festivals
could you attend? None! You would be sent home
in tears, without your share of holy joy.   1690
When the time comes to marry, my daughters,
what man will risk the revulsion—
the infamy!—that will wound you
just as it wounded your parents?
What evil is missing? Your father killed
his father. He had children with the mother
who bore him, fathered you
at the source of his own life.

                Those are the insults
you will face. Who will marry you?
No one, my children. You will grow old   1700
unmarried, living a dried-up childless life.
Kreon, you're all the father they have now.
The parents who conceived them are both lost.
Keep these two girls from rootless wandering—
unmarried and helpless. They are your kin.
Don't bring them down to what I am.
Pity them. They are so young, and but for you,
alone. Touch my hand, kind man,
make that touch your promise.

KREON touches him.

Children, had you been old enough   1710
to comprehend, I would have taught you more.

Now, all I can do is ask you to pray
that you live only where you're welcomed,
that your lives be happier than mine was—
the father from whose seed you were born.

KREON

Enough grief. Go inside now.

OEDIPUS

Bitter words that I must obey.

KREON

Time runs out on all things.

OEDIPUS

Grant my request before I go.

KREON

Speak.   1720

OEDIPUS

Banish me from my homeland.

KREON

Ask god to do that, not me.

OEDIPUS

I am the man the gods hate most.

KREON

Then you will have your wish.

OEDIPUS

You consent?

KREON

I never promise if I can't be sure.

OEDIPUS

Then lead me inside.

KREON

Come. Let go of your children now.

OEDIPUS

Don't take them from me.

KREON

Give up your power, too.   1730
You won the power once, but you couldn't
keep it to the end of your life.

KREON leads OEDIPUS into the palace.

LEADER

Thebans, that man is the same Oedipus
whose great mind solved the famous riddle.
He was a most powerful man.

Which of us seeing his glory, his prestige,
did not wish his luck could be ours?
Now look at what wreckage the seas
of savage trouble have made of his life.
To know the truth of a man, wait   1740
till you see his life end.
On that day, look at him.
Don't claim any man is god's friend
until he has passed through life
and crossed the border into death—
never having been god's victim.

ALL *leave.*

NOTES TO THE PLAY

1–7 *My children . . . Healing God?* These first lines in the Greek
are compressed—dense with mythic, dramatic, and ironic
significance. Oedipus emerges from the palace to confront a
sea of green branches—the olive boughs his agitated Theban
subjects have brought to him in supplication (see note to 4).
He plays on that image—"fresh green life / old Kadmos nurtures and protects"—to acknowledge the citizens' ancestry:
they are the latest crop, the newest descendants of Kadmos,
Thebes' legendary founder and its first king, who seeded the
ground with dragon's teeth from which sprang fully armed
soldiers. That Oedipus invokes Kadmos as the still-fathering
source of Thebes' newest generation registers the power en-
during paternal bloodlines held for fifth-century Greeks.
By referring to the delegation as *trophê*—an abstract noun
used here to mean "those cared for" or "those protected" by
Kadmos—Oedipus seems briefly to be puzzled as to why the
delegation appeals to him for help, rather than to the city's
divinities. He tries to shift responsibility for their welfare
away from himself to Kadmos. But the compassion he extends to them in his first words—by calling them his "children," as though he were related by blood—turns out to be

more than a metaphoric gesture when Oedipus discovers that Kadmos is his ancestor as well.

4 *with your wool-strung boughs* Suppliants left branches of laurel or olive, with tufts of wool tied on to them, at the altars of gods to whom they appealed for help. But here the use of suppliant boughs to seek help from a mortal man is highly unusual. Oedipus' initial puzzlement as to why he is being petitioned with ritual emblems of supplication also suggests his reluctance to get involved, perhaps his sense of inadequacy. This momentary doubt vanishes as he feels his subjects' need and as his strength and competence recover. He has indeed, we soon learn, been totally aware of Thebes' widespread devastation.

6–7 *prayers . . . Healing God* Literally, "paeans." A paean was a hymn to Apollo as a healer of disease, one of the god's many roles. Although the oracle that predicted the plague was given by Apollo—and Homer's *Iliad* tells us he could send a plague as well as cure one—nothing in the text implicates him as the cause of the plague now inflicting Thebes.

26–27 *river shrine . . . ashes . . . prophecy* Literally, "prophetic embers of Ismenos." A temple on the shores of the Ismenos, one of the two Theban rivers, was dedicated to Apollo. Embers in the temple smoldered under a sacrificed animal whose burnt remains could be read to interpret the will of a god, in this case Apollo's.

31 *Plague* The plague that had struck Thebes was general, destroying crops, animals, and people. The fiery heat characteristic of the fever is referred to again at 227–228 (see note

to 224–239). The resemblance between the plague in this play and the Athenian plague of 430 BCE as described by Thucydides has led some scholars to date the play shortly after 429. See especially Bernard Knox, "The Date of the *Oedipus Tyrannus* of Sophocles," in *American Journal of Philology* 77, no. 2 (1956).

34 *A burning god* The Greeks assumed a god to be responsible for a general and devastating plague. At 224 the Chorus names Ares, symbol of violence or destructiveness, as the responsible divinity.

37 *Hades* The god who presides over the underworld.

38–41 *We haven't come . . . confronting gods* The Priest explains why he, a man who himself has access to the gods, comes to Oedipus, a political leader, for help in this crisis; Oedipus has proven his ability to act effectively in situations requiring direct contact with a divinity.

42–44 *freed us . . . rasping Singer* The "rasping Singer" is the Sphinx, pictured by Greek artists of Sophocles' time with a lion's body, a woman's head and breasts, and wings. She arrived in Thebes shortly after Laios' departure and destroyed young Thebans ("the tax we paid with our lives") by posing a riddle that resulted in the death of those who answered incorrectly. (In some versions of the myth, the victims were thrown from a cliff, and in others they were strangled, perhaps in some sexual embrace; the word "Sphinx" is related to the Greek verb meaning "to strangle.") Oedipus triumphed by solving the riddle and killing the Sphinx, thus liberating Thebes from a reign of terror. One version of the riddle follows; it appears in myth in slightly different formulations: "There exists on land a thing with two feet and four feet, with a single voice, that has three feet as well. It changes shape alone among the things that move on land or in the air or down through the sea. Yet during periods when it is supported by the largest number of feet, then is the speed in its limbs the feeblest of all" (Gould 1970, 19). By answering "man," Oedipus demonstrated his lifelong attribute, intellectual resourcefulness in harrowing circumstances. Sophocles refrains from presenting the riddle itself, perhaps because its folk-tale cleverness seemed too insufficient a proof of real intelligence.

51 *god's intimation* A prophetic voice, an oracle or augury, or a divine signal of some kind.

62 *a bird from god* Birdlife was a major medium of communication between gods and mortals. Prophets and seers divined messages from birds' songs and flight patterns. Oedipus himself is ironically seen here as a favorable birdlike omen. See *Antigone*, note to 463–464.

62 *good luck* The first of many invocations of the Greek concept of *tyche*, which can mean "luck," "chance," or "fate." I generally translate "luck" when the speaker is gratified, "chance" when the outcome seems uncertain or unfortunate, and "fate" when a divinity seems involved.

69 *I know what need* Oedipus' grasp of the situation might seem contradictory to his initial professed ignorance of the suppliants' appeal. In his first speech, he was simply searching for new developments and urging his people to voice fears and needs. Here he reveals his continued concern and reports specific actions he has taken.

69 *this sickness* Oedipus refers both to the literal "sickness" of the suppliants, all victims in some respect of the plague, and to his own metaphoric sickness—his mental suffering for his fellow Thebans. But the Greek audience understood that the "sickness" that affects Oedipus, of which he is unaware, is not metaphoric at all but a literal pollution of his entire being. Sophocles will continue to reveal how characters' metaphoric speech turns out to be unexpectedly and horrifyingly literal.

81 *Phoibos* Apollo.

85 *He takes too long* The Pythoness at Delphi delivered answers to questioners only once a month, and the shortest possible elapsed time for a trip from Thebes to Delphi and back would be about four or five days.

90 *Lord Apollo* This exclamation could be as much an impromptu prayer as an oath. The stage might contain a statue of Apollo to which Oedipus turns or nods as he speaks these lines.

91–92 *Luck so bright . . . see it* I follow the interpretation of these lines given by Lowell Edmunds in "Sophocles' *Oedipus Tyrannus*," in *Harvard Studies in Classical Philology* 80–81 (1976): 41–44, who disputes the traditional interpretation: "May his radiant look prove the herald of good news." Arguing that Sophocles uses an idiom dependent on a suppressed preposition, Edmunds believes *eu* should be understood before *ommati* and the lines literally be translated as "May he come bright with saving fortune as he is bright to view."

laurel crown A laurel crown customarily signified that a pilgrimage to a shrine or an oracle had been a success.

96 *Menoikeos* One of the "Sown Men" who grew up instantly and fully armed in Thebes when Kadmos seeded the earth with dragon's teeth. Pronounced "Me-NEE-kius."

98–99 *A good one . . . will be fine* A deliberately obscure answer. Kreon here resists revealing, until directed by Oedipus, the shocking nature of the oracle he has received. The lines also suggest Kreon's annoying use of a Sophist's quibbling idiom.

102–103 *in front . . . go inside* Kreon gives Oedipus the option of keeping Thebes in the dark about the oracle's disturbing accusations.

107 *very clear* Kreon remarks on the lack of evasion or surface difficulty in this new oracle. Oracles (frequently delivered in lines of hexameter verse) were sometimes cryptic and demanded interpretation. The oracles to Oedipus are among the rare ones in Greek myth that mean exactly what they literally say.

113 *banishing . . . killing* Apollo offers Thebes two choices for purging itself of Laios' murderer: death or exile. This choice comes up again when Oedipus charges Kreon with the crime and when Oedipus and Kreon debate Oedipus' ultimate fate.

113–114 *blood— / kin murder* The presence in a city of a person who had shed the blood of someone in his own family was absolutely horrifying and unacceptable to a Greek. Even in the late fifth century, lawyers made dramatic use of this horror when prosecuting murderers.

120 *own hands* The first of many references to hands, especially hands that shed blood. In Greek law the hands of a person

who committed a crime retained the pollution inherent in that crime, regardless of motive or intent. Here Oedipus' avenging hands are paired rhetorically with the hands that murdered Laios. The two pairs of hands will be shown to be only one pair, Oedipus' own.

129–130 *journey . . . god's presence* The Greek word so translated is *theoros*, literally, a spectator of (or witness to) a divine rite or event. We know from Euripides' *Phoenician Women* (Grene and Lattimore, vol. IV, 1959, 462) that Laios was on his way to Delphi to ask the Pythoness whether or not the son he had exposed was really dead. But by not specifically naming Laios' destination, Sophocles permits Oedipus to postpone facing the possibility that Laios and he were traveling on the same road at the same time.

141 *bandit* Though Kreon clearly used the plural in 138, Oedipus speaks of a single bandit with chilling, unconscious accuracy. But because his sentence is a hypothetical question, it is logically proper.

144–145 *new troubles . . . no avenger* Kreon evokes a rapid sequence of events: Laios' departure; news of his death; attack by the Sphinx; arrival of Oedipus; death of the Sphinx. The elapsed time might have been only a few days, or at most a week or two.

147 *blocked* The Greek word so translated, *empodon*, refers to stumbling, tripping, or impeding the legs.

150 *at our feet* Kreon continues the foot imagery, which may carry a reference to Oedipus' own swollen feet.

160 *exacting vengeance* Oedipus strangely imagines himself the victim of a second crime by Laios' original murderer. That this should be an act of "vengeance" is hard to explain given

the state of Oedipus' knowledge, but it will indeed be an act of vengeance when the same hands that killed Laios blind Oedipus.

164 *people of Kadmos* Theban citizens. When they arrive, the Chorus will represent the "people of Kadmos."

173 *Voice from Zeus* Though Apollo was the resident deity who issued his prophecies through the Pythoness at Delphi, the Chorus here attributes the commands to Zeus, the ultimate source of knowledge and power.

179 *Delos* The island at the center of the Cyclades, birthplace of Apollo, was said to be the navel of the sea, as Delphi was the navel of the Earth. Gods communicated with mortals through both connections.

181 *new threat . . . old doom* The Chorus distinguishes between a curse that has been known for some years and one that has newly emerged. The Voice of Zeus will invoke an old curse against the murderer of Laios.

186–191 *Athena . . . Artemis . . . Apollo* The Chorus, not knowing which god will be the truly relevant one, prays to three divinities to focus their powers on rescuing Thebes.

208 *Deathgod* Hades.

224–239 *Ares . . . who kills us* The war god Ares is not associated with the plague in myth, but Sophocles probably alludes to the plague's spread in Athens during the Spartan attacks of 430–425. The image of Ares as a murderer "without armor now" reflects the fifth-century Greeks' lack of knowledge about infectious diseases. Throngs of rural Greeks, assuming Athens a safe haven from the Spartans, flocked to the city; there the overcrowded conditions facilitated the plague's swift and deadly spread. In Aeschylus' *Suppliants* (Grene and Lattimore, vol. I, 1959, 201), Ares personifies the plague or destruction itself.

229–230 *vast sea-room / of Amphitritê* Literally, "great hall of Amphitritê." Amphitritê was a sea nymph whose home was the Atlantic Ocean, hence her name became synonymous with that body of water.

232 *jagged harbors* Literally, "welcomeless anchorage."

233 *seas off Thrace* The Black Sea. The Thracians, who lived on its shores, were warlike; Ares was their primary god.

233–235 *If night . . . finish it* The meaning is obscure, but Gould (1970, 39) suggests "if the night lets anything survive, the day moves in to finish it."

240 *lord of the morning light* Literally, "Lycean Lord." Lycean was one of Apollo's epithets and could suggest either "light" or "wolf." The Chorus surely calls on him here in his protective, light-bringing aspect.

246 *morning hills* Literally, "Lycian hills," in southwestern Asia Minor, where Artemis was worshipped, with her brother Apollo, as a fire deity. Sophocles puns on the similarity between Lycean and Lycian to stress the light-bringing character of the sibling gods.

250 *Bakkhos* An alternate name for Dionysos, the god of wine and other forms of intoxication and ecstasy. He was a native Theban, the son of Zeus and Semele, Kadmos' daughter.

251 *maenads* Literally, "madwomen." Revelers loyal to Dionysos.

263 *I'm a stranger* According to Athenian law, a blood relative of a slain person should act to interdict the murderer. Unknowingly, Oedipus is in fact such a relative, though here he acts as a representative of the state speaking for the next of kin, who is presumed to be absent.

265 *mesh some clue* The word translated as "clue" is *symbolon*, a fragment of some larger object, typically a potsherd. When matched to fit its other half, it established the identity of a messenger or long-lost parent or relative.

268 *come late* Oedipus arrived in Thebes after the report of Laios' death had reached the city.

273 *Labdakos* An earlier king of Thebes.

286–289 *roof . . . speak . . . pray . . . sacrifice . . . pour* The prohibitions in Oedipus' decree reveal the extreme aversion felt by a Greek of Sophocles' time to any contact with a person whose hands had committed a defiling act. See *Kolonos*, note to 1029.

316–317 *Laios / had no luck . . . children* An example of words whose second meaning will be grasped when the true facts of Oedipus' life are known. Oedipus means to say that Laios was childless, but the words also suggest that any child Laios fathered was the *source* of his ill fortune.

318 *came down on his head* This idiom through which Oedipus explains Laios' death is uncannily appropriate to the way in which Laios actually died: from a blow to the head, struck by Oedipus himself.

324 *all our kings* My gloss added to explain Oedipus' list.

335 *None of us is the killer* The blunt denial is understandable, because Oedipus has addressed the Chorus as if it potentially harbored Laios' killer.

343 *Tiresias* The blind Theban prophet, who figures in many of the most famous myths of his native city. His association with the god Apollo, and his access to the god's knowledge, are crucial here, because Apollo is the source of the oracles that predicted Oedipus' incest and patricide.

348 *Kreon's urging* An important point. Later, when Tiresias accuses Oedipus of causing the pollution, Oedipus remembers that it was Kreon who advised consulting the seer. Kreon's involvement thus lends plausibility to Oedipus' countercharges.

352 *travelers* The Leader substitutes a word that is nearer the truth than Kreon's "bandits." Oedipus does not react to the difference.

354 *who did it* Here I accept an anonymous emendation cited by Burton in Jebb (1883, 50). The manuscripts literally say "the one who saw it no one sees." But the emendation fits the context of the next three speeches, which concern not the eyewitness, but the killer, the one who did it.

390–391 *lawful . . . guidance* Greek cities were morally, if not legally, entitled to benefit from the wisdom of an acknowledged prophet. Here, at first, Oedipus' remonstrance is gentle. (See Jebb 1883, 54.)

393–394 *What you've said . . . happen to me* Tiresias refers here most probably to the part of Oedipus' speech that curses Laios' murderer. Less probably, he might be referring to the plea with which Oedipus greets him. The manuscripts contain a possible variant of these lines, which Gould translates, "I see your understanding comes to you inopportunely. So that won't happen to me . . ." (1970, 54). This variant makes sense in the larger context of Oedipus' discovery of his true

past. I have, however, translated the line to make the most
sense in the immediate context.

399 *You know and won't help?* Tiresias' scornful refusal to
respond seems not only inexplicable to Oedipus but unacceptable. Tiresias must be made to tell what the city needs
to know for its survival. Oedipus' fury may be justified as
necessary to force the truth from him.

406 *rage* A cunning double meaning. Tiresias speaks of "rage"
(*orgei*, a feminine noun in Greek) as something Oedipus
"cohabits" or "dwells" with and of which he is ignorant.
Oedipus thinks he is being accused of possessing a violent
nature. But because this "rage" is also spoken of as a sexual
partner, Tiresias' words could mean as well that Oedipus is
ignorant of the identity of his own wife. Sophocles has the
Messenger describe the last frantic actions of Jokasta, after
she knows Oedipus is her son, as *orge*, or raging (1406).
The characterization of Oedipus' whole family by its rage is
prominent in Aeschylus and even earlier writers.

425–426 *charge . . . flushed out* The metaphor is from hunting and suggests, first, that the accusation is like an animal
driven from its cover and, second, that Tiresias himself has
become an animal fleeing Oedipus' wrath.

440–441 *living . . . intimacy* This phrase normally means "to
live under the same roof," but it also frequently means
"to have sexual intercourse with."

442 *nearest and most loving kin* The most frequent reference of
this phrase (*philatoi*) is to one's blood kin; less often it refers
to those whom one loves, regardless of blood relationship.
Tiresias' lines seem to Oedipus an astonishing insult because

their true import, that his wife is his closest blood relative, is unthinkable. See introduction to *Antigone*, passim.

451 *You can't harm me* This phrase could also mean "I shall not harm you." My translation is governed by acceptance of Brunck's emendation in the next speech, as cited in Jebb (1883, 61).

453 *I'm not the one who will bring you down* All but one of the manuscripts give, "It's not my fate to be struck down by you." If this version is sound, the rest of Tiresias' speech makes little sense. If, however, Brunck's emendation of a fourteenth-century manuscript is correct, as most modern editors believe, Apollo's involvement in Oedipus' downfall follows quite logically.

455 *Or was it Kreon?* In seeking an explanation for what he sees as false and treasonous accusations by Tiresias, Oedipus connects Kreon's recommendation to call in Tiresias with the fact that banishing Oedipus would leave Kreon in position to assume the throne. This sudden accusation against Kreon suggests not only Oedipus' quick mind, but the suspiciousness and ruthless initiative required of a *tyrannos* (see note to 1006–1007). Gould has drawn a useful distinction between Tiresias and Oedipus under duress (1970, 60). While Oedipus sharpens his ability to make inferences, Tiresias can only clarify and elaborate on Oedipus' guilt with an intuitive vision. The prophet is unreasonable but correct, Oedipus plausible but wrong.

465 *bogus beggar-priest* The Greeks used the word *magus* to refer to what they considered an unreliable and corruptible breed of fortune-tellers from Persia.

476 *the know-nothing* Oedipus himself stresses the difference between his ability to solve problems intellectually and Tiresias' failure to solve them using the arts of prophecy. Oedipus smugly boasts of his "ignorance" but is in fact truly and desperately ignorant of the hidden facts that will ruin him.

506 *terror-stricken feet* The phrase may mean that the curse pursuing Oedipus is itself "terrible footed." But the sound of the word for "terrible footed," *deinopous*, echoes Oedipus' name (literally, "Swollenfoot") so as to suggest that Oedipus' scarred feet, which were pinned together when he was exposed at birth, are in some way terrible or terrified.

511 *Kithairon* The mountain on which Oedipus, as an infant, was left to die.

517 *bring you down to what you are* This sentence is obscure in Greek. Jebb suggests that it means Oedipus will be leveled, i.e., "equal" to his true self by being revealed as Laios' son, and "equal" to his own children, all of whom have the same mother, Jokasta (1883, 67).

520 *warning spoken through my mouth* This seeming circumlocution conveys the fact that Tiresias is not the source of his prophecies, but the transmitter of Apollo's messages. The word *stoma*, or "mouth," also means the message spoken by the mouth.

531 *Who was my father?* Literally, "the one who gave me birth." The word is masculine, indicating that Oedipus asks who his male parent is.

557 *father's seed and his seed* Literally, "seed fellow to his father." The word *homosporos* names one who impregnates the same woman as his father, but it also carries the suggestion of blood relationship to the father.

571 *Fates* The *Keres*, who execute the will of Zeus and Apollo.

574 *Parnassos* The mountain home of the Muses, visible from Thebes.

582 *Earth . . . mouth* Literally, "from Earth's mid-navel." The navel was a white stone at Delphi, at the spot where oracles or "dooms" such as those mentioned here were spoken. The navel, or *omphalos*, was an avenue of communication to the wisdom of the earth. See note to 179.

585 *man who reads birds* Tiresias.

589–597 *doubt . . . no proof* The Chorus faces a hard choice. Either they must abandon their trust in divine oracles or they must accuse Oedipus of the death of Laios. They decide that before joining with Tiresias, they must have some proof (literally, a "touchstone," *basanos*, which streaks black when rubbed with true gold) to remove their doubt. Because no metaphoric touchstone exists—no feud or crime that set the Korinthian royal house against the Theban House of Kadmos—they withhold their accusation.

608–609 *charges / proved against him* Here again the word "touchstone" is used, this time as a verb.

637 *master's murderer* Oedipus' language is perhaps purposely ambiguous. He proleptically accuses Kreon of murdering him, but the phrase could accuse Kreon of Laios' murder.

664 *Laios?* Kreon has not yet heard Tiresias' charges, hence his surprise.

671 *hunt down the killer* Oedipus may be hinting that the investigation of Laios' murder was less than thorough.

688 *rationally* Kreon's pedantic reasonableness contrasts sharply with Oedipus' impatient quickness. His laborious

catalog of the disadvantages of kingship may be heartfelt, but its pompous rhetorical expression generates suspicion in Oedipus.

696 *To be king* These protestations should be compared with Kreon's later implicit acceptance of the kingship at 1730–1732.

707 *Nor would I join someone* This oblique reference is probably to Tiresias. Kreon accepts the possibility that Tiresias is treasonous in his accusations; he clearly does not believe such accusations against Oedipus to be valid.

732 *your death* Oedipus chooses the harsher penalty of the two, death or exile, that the Delphi oracle promised Kreon would cure Thebes at 113. But Oedipus may have in mind that execution was the normal punishment for treason.

733 *Then start by defining "betrayal"* The text, in the judgment of many scholars, may be corrupt at this point. Editors have attempted to preserve continuous sense by reassigning the lines to other speakers and by positing a line to bridge the gap in logic after Gr. 625 (734). Gould, however, argues plausibly that Kreon's proclivity for verbal analysis and Socratic love of general laws may explain his apparent non sequitur, which attempts to deflect Oedipus from violence into philosophical debate (1970, 84). I accept Gould's defense of the manuscripts and translate the text as received.

755 *or to have me killed* Kreon reverts to the choice of banishment or death proposed by the oracle he himself brought from Delphi. He also may have assumed Oedipus' recent threat of death to be hyperbole.

757 *False prophecy* Literally, "evil arts." This implies that Kreon has employed Tiresias to make false charges disguised as prophecy to destroy Oedipus. Such treacherous use of prophecy was a part of fifth-century Greek political life.

758 *I ask the gods* Kreon makes a formal declaration of innocence that invokes the gods; his innocence is instantly respected as valid by all but Oedipus.

763–812 *Give in . . . luck* These lines are a *kommos*, a sung expression of grief or strong emotion in which the Leader joins one or more of the main characters. To judge by the root meaning of *kommos* (which is "beat"), this portion must have had a more strongly accented rhythm than the rest of the dialogue. Here the emotion might stem from the realization, by all present, of increasingly grave circumstances.

775 *No! We ask neither* Though the Chorus reveres Oedipus for the success and prosperity of his kingship, it does not accept either of the harsh alternatives his quick mind suggests: Oedipus sees that if Kreon's conspiracy is not stamped out, it will lead ultimately to his own destruction. The Chorus gropes for a less severe outcome and gradually refrains from identifying with Oedipus as the events of his life are revealed to them.

776 *the Sun* The Sun frequently appears as the source of final appeal in tragedy, as it will later at 1617 when Kreon orders Oedipus out of its "life-giving flame."

782 *let him go* That Oedipus yields, however grudgingly, shows that his stubbornness and self-confidence are not immune to persuasion, nor is he insensitive to the wishes of those close to him.

818 *He says I murdered Laios* Kreon did not say this, of course. Because Oedipus so passionately believes in the truth of his inference—that Kreon is responsible for Tiresias' charges—he puts Tiresias' words in Kreon's mouth.

827 *I don't say Apollo himself sent it* This qualification both absolves Apollo from false prophecy and expresses skepticism concerning oracles, skepticism that must have been shared widely in a world where oracles were constantly put to dubious political use. The Chorus has the strongest commitment to the divine authority of oracles. Oedipus' belief is conditioned by experience and changes with events.

829–830 *destined to die / at the hands of* In Jokasta's version, the oracle to Laios was unqualified and not meant as a punishment. Gould notes that by omitting the aspect of punishment present in earlier versions of the myth, Sophocles establishes the pure and unexplained malice of Apollo's destruction of Oedipus.

832 *three roads meet* This is the detail that disturbs Oedipus, and the one he reverts to as soon as Jokasta ends her speech. The actor playing Oedipus must make a gesture of recognition to account for Jokasta's question at 846. Sophocles might have meant such a pointed reaction to explain why Oedipus was distracted from picking up another fact with direct bearing on his identity: Jokasta's child's feet had been "pierced and pinned" together, as Oedipus' own had been, to produce the swollen scars that gave him his name. However, the weight to be given Oedipus' crippled feet may not be as conclusive as some commentators think. If exposure of children was common, Oedipus might not be expected

to connect himself instantly and absolutely with Laios' son, even if he had heard Jokasta's words.

841–843 *god wants . . . showing what he's done* Literally, "Of what things the god hunts the use, he reveals easily himself." Allusions to hunting appear also at 267, 426, and 671. The words here conjure the image of god seizing his prey and then displaying it.

846 *What fear made you turn* Jokasta could refer either to a movement by Oedipus at 844–845 or earlier, at 832.

851–852 *Phokis . . . Daulis* Towns near Delphi.

854 *before you came to power* For the sequence of events leading to Oedipus' assumption of power in Thebes, see the introduction to the play.

858 *Was he a young man* Oedipus poses as the first alternative the one he must hope is true: that Laios was not an older man of an age to be his father. In her response, Jokasta not only dashes this hope but suggests a physical resemblance between Laios and Oedipus.

862 *that savage curse* Oedipus declared this interdiction against Laios' murderer at 290–303.

869 *a herald* The presence of a herald might have indicated to Oedipus that the party contained a prince or ruler.

876 *touched . . . begged* A touch on the arm, like clasping a person's knees, was a formal supplication, an appeal to piety in hope of achieving a favorable response.

883 *I've said too much* What Oedipus means here is uncertain. Most likely, as Gould suggests, he regrets the curse pronounced against himself—the curse to which he has already referred at 862 (1970, 98).

890 *know the risks* Literally, "while I cross through this chance [*tyche*]."

891–892 *Polybos . . . Merope* Are we to understand that Oedipus has never before named his parents or his origins to Jokasta? Although such extreme reticence is possible, it is much more likely that Sophocles uses here an epic convention whereby a hero begins a piece of consequential autobiography by formally naming his homeland and immediate ancestors.

893–894 *Chance . . . blow* An excellent instance of Sophocles' practice of having Oedipus label as chance or luck an event that, seen in retrospect, becomes part of the pattern of his ruin created by Apollo.

904 *the rumor still rankled; it hounded me* The Greek word *hupheppe* could mean either that the rumor "crept abroad" or that "the memory recurred." I have tried to translate the phrase so as to include both possibilities.

905 *with no word to my parents* Had Oedipus informed his parents of the mission to Delphi, they presumably would have intervened. By seeking assurance of his birth beyond his parents' word, Oedipus placed himself in the hands of the god Apollo. It was both a conventional and a rational act, because Delphi could serve as a locator of lost kin, and because Oedipus had no reason to suspect the god held any enmity toward him.

907 *god would not honor me* What was the question Oedipus put to the Pythoness? "Who are my true parents?" or "Is Polybos my true father?" For the oracle not to answer such a question seems to Oedipus a violation of the normal

treatment a pilgrim could expect from the god (literally, "Phoibos," or Apollo) at Delphi.

909–910 *his words flashed . . . horrible, wretched things* The phrase is so vivid some scholars have questioned its authenticity. It does fit both Oedipus' present mental condition, in which he sees himself as a target for strange malice, and the verbs of leaping and striking that Sophocles uses for actions attributable to Apollo. The oracle given Oedipus is not an answer to his question, but an attack on Oedipus—not a clarification, but a condemnation that impacts Oedipus with a shock or flash. His reaction, to flee Korinth and his parents, is entirely comprehensible and in no way morally flawed. An oracle might be fulfilled in a metaphorical or oblique manner; in real life, some oracles were never fulfilled, a frequent event in the experience of Sophocles' audience. In tragedy, however, the audience would expect all oracles to be completed. Many readers think that Oedipus ought eventually to have considered the oracle's broader implications. (Could the oracle be telling me that Polybos is not my father? Had I better avoid killing anyone old enough to be my father or marrying a woman old enough to be my mother?) But Sophocles gave his audience no opportunity in the play's swift action to consider such questions; the speed with which he shows us the oracle's completion fits with the consistent image of the god leaping or striking at Oedipus.

926 *man out front* Presumably the herald.

929–936 *I smash . . . kill them all* Oedipus uses the historical present tense in these lines. Although the events happened some twenty years earlier, they are vivid and immediate in his mind (Segal 2001, 90).

933–934 *staff / this hand holds* The hand was the instrument that retained the defilement of its acts. The actor might have raised his hand at this point, as he might have at other times when his hand is named. In Athenian law, acts committed by an agent's own hand, even if involuntarily, resulted in pollution, but masterminding or delegating the act escaped such stigma.

936 *kill them all* Said in pride, perhaps, but not in boastfulness. Laios' men would have attacked him; only by killing or disabling all would he have survived. In fact, Oedipus killed only four; the fifth (the herald) escaped, or perhaps recovered from a wound after being left for dead.

937 *stranger and Laios . . . were the same blood* In Greek, the word for stranger, *xenos*, could apply to Oedipus himself.

938 *triumph* The Greek word so translated is *athlios*, a superlative form of *athlon*, a contest or combat.

949 *utter filth* The Greek word so translated is *anagnos*, meaning "guilty," "unclean," or "unholy," and is usually translated as "polluted," which I avoid to escape confusion with modern uses of that word.

955 *brought me up and gave me birth* By reversing the natural order—birth followed by nurture— Sophocles reminds us that Polybos "gave birth" to Oedipus only by bringing him up and falsely claiming him as his own son.

965 *eyewitness* Literally, "person who was there."

976 *braving the road alone* The Greek word here is somewhat mysterious and might be translated literally as "with solitary

belt." The word appears nowhere else in surviving Greek. It may mean simply "dressed as a traveler."

978 *evidence will drag me down* Literally, "the balance tips toward me." The metaphor is from scales for weighing, a typical one in judicial contexts. See *Oedipus at Kolonos*, note to 1652.

986 *poor doomed child* Literally, "unhappy person" (*dystanos*). Here Jokasta is thinking of the short, doomed life of her baby and uses the most common word for "unfortunate one." In her final speeches to Oedipus (at 1214 and 1217), she will use the same word to sum up his life.

989 *look right, then left* Literally, "shoot frightened glances right and left" (Gould 1970, 106). Ancient Greeks, who habitually took actions and made decisions based on signs and omens from the divinities, interpreted the sudden presence of a person or bird as hopeful (if it appeared on the right) and dangerous (if it appeared on the left). Jokasta has abandoned such precautions.

996 *sky-walking laws* Literally, "sky-footed." The laws to which the Chorus refers here are those whose origins go as far back as human consciousness does, laws inseparable from our instinctive behavior. The laws forbidding incest and kin murder would be those most on the Chorus's mind.

1006–1007 *A violent will / fathers the tyrant* Literally, "*hubris* plants the seed of the *tyrannos*." *Hubris*, a general word for violence, outrage, and moral insubordination, sums up the actions of a person who exercises pure will without constraint, and thus applies most exactly to a Greek *tyrannos*.

The name *tyrannos* was given to powerful rulers from the late seventh to the early fifth centuries who "emerged from the aristocratic oligarchy as sole rulers of their city-states, responsible only to themselves. . . . They were necessarily energetic, intelligent, confident, ambitious, and aggressive; they also had to be ruthless and suspicious of plots to overthrow their sometimes precarious position" (Segal 2001, 6). The term did not acquire our pejorative meaning of "tyrant" until Plato, in the fourth century. Throughout the play Sophocles uses *tyrannos* in the more neutral sense of a *basileus*, or king, except at 1007, where the modern sense of the tyrant is surely intended.

1039–1041 *Delphi . . . Olympia . . . Abai* All are holy shrines and destinations of religious pilgrimages. See note to 179.

1049 *the gods lose force* Literally, "the things pertaining to divinity slowly depart."

1080 *isthmus* The Isthmus of Korinth connects the Peloponnesus to the Greek mainland.

1104 *scour Pythian smoke* Literally, "scrutinize the Pythian hearth." The Pythoness delivered the prophecies from within a basement cell inside the temple of Apollo in Delphi, located on the slopes of Mount Parnassos. The smoky vapors that rose from the temple floor were reputed to put her in a trance. Recent geological studies of the soil around Delphi suggest that the fumes from its underlying rock structure contained ethylene—a sweet-smelling gas, once used as an anesthetic, that produces a pleasant euphoria. (See William J. Broad, "For Delphic Oracle, Fumes and Visions," *New York Times,* 19 March 2002, late ed.: F1.)

1131 *shines a great light* Literally, "great eye." The Greeks believed eyes projected powerful rays toward the people and the objects they looked at. Other uses of this metaphor in Greek literature suggest that a "great eye" was a sign of wonderful good hope or good luck.

1155 *unforgivable harm* Literally, "Lest you receive a religious pollution from those who planted you."

1214 *You poor child!* Jokasta calls Oedipus *dystanos*, the same word she called her child who was exposed and presumed dead (see note to 986). She now knows that child is Oedipus, and will call him *dystanos* once more at 1217. In his next speech, Oedipus will disclaim all human mothering and claim Luck (*Tyche*) for his parent (1226); he sees only the good in his situation at the moment.

1248 *Pan* A god holy to rural people, Pan was a patron of shepherds and herdsmen, as well as a fertility god amorous to both sexes. The mountain he roves is Kithairon, the mountain on which Oedipus' parents instructed the shepherd to let him die.

1253–1256 *Hermes . . . Kyllene . . . Helikon* Like Pan, Hermes was a god well known to country people for playing childish tricks. Zeus made him his messenger and gave him the wide-brimmed hat, winged sandals, and *kerykeion* (or *caduceus* in Latin, meaning herald's staff) with which he is often shown. Because of his association with roads, Hermes is known as the patron of wayfarers—traders, travelers, and thieves. The Chorus's mention of him might allude to the crossroads, the place at which Oedipus killed Laios. Kyllene, a haunt of both Pan and

Hermes, is a mountain in Arcadia in the central Peloponnesus, the largest peninsula south of Attica, connected to the mainland only by the Isthmus of Korinth. The Muses inhabited a sanctuary on Helikon, a mountain south of Thebes.

1288 *Arcturos* A star near the Big Dipper that, when it appeared in September, signaled the end of summer in Greece.

1326 *Kill her own child?* The Greek phrase so translated, *tlemon tekousa* (literally, "poor woman, she who gave birth"), "shows how difficult it is to translate Sophocles' density and richness of meaning" (Segal 2001, 103). Here Sophocles implies that Jokasta found herself doing something utterly horrible for a mother to do: killing her own child.

1350 *Your fate teaches* Literally, "with your example [or "paradigm," *paradigmos*] before us."

1351–1352 *the story / god spoke* Literally, "with your *daimon* before us." See the introduction to this play for a discussion of *daimon*.

1358 *who sang the god's dark oracles* Literally, "singer of oracles." Presumably a reference to the Sphinx's riddles, but the word "oracle" usually refers to divinely sanctioned responses such as those given by Delphi. Sophocles may here be connecting the Sphinx to the other instances of divine intervention in Oedipus' life.

1371 *tumbling* The Greek word so translated, *pesein*, literally means to "fall on," or "attack," and can refer in one usage to a baby falling between the legs of a woman squatted or seated in childbirth. E. A. Havelock (in Gould 1970, 138) suggests another meaning for the verb—to mount sexually,

in which case there is an overtone of violence. A variation of
the same verb, *empiptein*, used at 1431, I translate as "burst
into" to describe Oedipus' entry into Jokasta's bedroom
after she's committed suicide. (See also note for 1419.)

1391 *Danube . . . Rion* The river Danube was called the Ister in
the ancient world. The Rion, the modern name of the Phasis,
is a river in the Caucasus, on the edge of what was then the
known world.

1394 *not involuntary evil. It was willed* The Servant refers to
Jokasta's suicide and Oedipus' self-blinding; he contrasts
these conscious and willed actions with the ones Jokasta
and Oedipus made without understanding their true con-
sequences, such as their own marriage. Although Oedipus
knew what he was doing when he blinded himself, the action was just as fated as the patricide and incest; Tiresias
had predicted Oedipus' blindness earlier. When the Servant
says that voluntary evils are more painful, he cannot mean
that they are more blameworthy or more serious but that
they are done in horror and desperation—in contrast to the
earlier evils, such as the marriage, committed in optimism
and confidence.

1415 *doubled lives* The reference is to Oedipus' "double" (*diplos*)
relationship to Jokasta, as her son and husband. The word
appears again at 1429 with a comparable allusion, as Oedipus
enters the "double doors" of their bedroom. Another significant image of doubled action appears in the piercing of Oedipus' ankles and the striking out of his own eyes.

1419 *burst in* The Greek word so translated is *eisepaiein*, an unusual compound (from *eis*, "into," and *paiein*, "to strike")

that might have been a colloquial word for intercourse recognizable by the audience (Gould 1970, 47). It is used here to compare Oedipus' violent action to a sexual attack, and thus to link it both to incest and to parricide.

1424–1425 *furrowed twice-mothering Earth . . . children sprang* The Messenger reports that Oedipus identifies Jokasta with an *aroura*, or furrowed field, as the source or origin of both Oedipus himself and the children he conceived with her. The image of Mother Earth figures significantly in the *Kolonos*. (See *Kolonos*, lines 1818–1820, and its introduction, p. 6.)

1431 *burst into* Again, the word *empiptein* (see note to 1371), used to refer to Oedipus' violation of Jokasta's "harbor" and her "furrow."

1512–1514 *Apollo . . . made evil, consummate evil / out of my life* Literally, "it was Apollo, friends, Apollo who brought to completion these, my evils [*pathea*]." A *pathos* (singular) is here, as often in Greek literature, an unmerited suffering sent by a god.

1516 *these eyes* Sophocles uses a pronoun (*nin*) for eyes, not a noun, and one that is the same for any gender, plural, dual, or singular. The ambiguity is surely deliberate but cannot be translated. Its inclusiveness, however, implies that *all* the blows that made his life evil, though struck by Oedipus himself, were caused by Apollo.

1724 *you will have your wish* Some scholars believe that Kreon is agreeing to Oedipus' plea to be exiled. But it is more likely that the words are noncommittal in the usual way of politicians.

1733–1746 *Thebans . . . god's victim* Some scholars question the authenticity of these lines, partly because of the difficulty in making sense of several of them, and partly because of their suspicious resemblance to the ending of Euripides' *Phoenician Women*. Modern audiences object to them mainly because they seem less than climactic. This objection is illegitimate. Greek dramatists did not place strong emphasis on concluding lines the way modern dramatists do, but often used them to facilitate the departure of the Chorus.

1746 *never having been god's victim* Literally, "having been made to undergo no anguish." The final word of the play, *pathon*, "having been made to undergo," is the same noun used at 1471 in a phrase I translate as "pure, helpless anguish." Oedipus also used *pathos* at 1513 when he explained that Apollo was the god who reduced him to misery. The word is often used as a technical phrase for the suffering of the *heros* in hero cults. The Latin translation is *passio*, which gives us in its Christian context the "passion" of Christ. The word appears in the concluding lines of two of Aeschylus' plays, *The Libation Bearers* and *Prometheus Bound*, as well as in the last sentence of Sophocles' *Elektra*. It does not figure in the conclusion of any of Euripides' surviving plays.

WORKS CITED AND CONSULTED

Aeschylus. *The Complete Greek Tragedies*. Trans. Richmond Lattimore, ed. David Grene and Richmond Lattimore. Chicago: University of Chicago Press, 1959.

Aristotle. *Aristotle's Poetics*. Trans. Leon Golden. Tallahassee: Florida State University Press, 1981.

———. *The Art of Rhetoric*. Trans. John Henry Freese. Loeb Classical Library 193. Cambridge, MA: Harvard University Press, 1967.

Berlin, Normand. *The Secret Cause: A Discussion of Tragedy*. Amherst: University of Massachusetts Press, 1981.

Blundell, Mary Whitlock. *Helping Friends and Harming Enemies: A Study in Sophocles and Greek Ethics*. Cambridge: Cambridge University Press, 1989.

Boegehold, Alan L. *When a Gesture Was Expected*. Princeton, NJ: Princeton University Press, 1999.

Carpenter, Thomas H., and Christopher A. Faraone, eds. *Masks of Dionysus*. Ithaca, NY: Cornell University Press, 1993.

Cartledge, Paul. *Ancient Greek Political Thought in Practice*. Cambridge: Cambridge University Press, 2009.

Csapo, Eric. *Actors and Icons of the Ancient Theater*. West Sussex, UK: Wiley-Blackwell, 2000.

Csapo, Eric, and William J. Slater. *The Context of Ancient Drama*. Ann Arbor: University of Michigan Press, 1994.

Davidson, John N. *Courtesans and Fishcakes: The Consuming Passions of Classical Athens*. New York: St. Martin's Press, 1998.

Easterling, P. E., ed. *The Cambridge Companion to Greek Tragedy*. Cambridge: Cambridge University Press, 1997.

Edmunds, Lowell. *Theatrical Space and Historical Place in Sophocles' "Oedipus at Colonus."* Lanham, MD: Rowman & Littlefield, 1996.

Else, Gerald F. *The Origin and Early Form of Greek Tragedy*. New York: Norton, 1965.

Euripides. *Euripides*. The Complete Greek Tragedies, vol. 4. Ed. David Grene and Richmond Lattimore. Chicago: University of Chicago Press, 1959.

Foley, Helene P. *Female Acts in Greek Tragedy*. Princeton, NJ: Princeton University Press, 2001.

Garland, Robert. *The Greek Way of Death*. Ithaca, NY: Cornell University Press, 1985.

———. *The Greek Way of Life*. Ithaca, NY: Cornell University Press, 1990.

Goldhill, Simon. *Reading Greek Tragedy*. Cambridge: Cambridge University Press, 1986.

Goldhill, Simon, and Edith Hall. *Sophocles and the Greek Tragic Tradition*. Cambridge: Cambridge University Press, 2009.

Gould, Thomas. *The Ancient Quarrel Between Poetry and Philosophy*. Princeton, NJ: Princeton University Press, 1990.

————, trans. *"Oedipus the King": A Translation with Commentary.* By Sophocles. Englewood Cliffs, NJ: Prentice-Hall, 1970.

Grene, David, trans. *Sophocles 1.* 2nd ed. The Complete Greek Tragedies. Ed. David Grene and Richmond Lattimore. Chicago: University of Chicago Press, 1991.

Guthrie, W. K. C. *The Greeks and Their Gods.* Boston: Beacon Press, 1950.

Hanson, Victor Davis. *A War Like No Other.* New York: Random House, 2005.

Herodotus. *The Landmark Herodotus: The Histories.* Ed. Robert B. Strassler. New York: Pantheon Books, 2007.

Hughes, Bettany. *The Hemlock Cup: Socrates, Athens and the Search for the Good Life.* New York: Knopf, 2010.

Jebb, R. C., trans. *Oedipus Tyrannus.* By Sophocles. Cambridge: Cambridge University, 1883.

Kagan, Donald. *Pericles of Athens and the Birth of Democracy.* New York: Touchstone–Simon & Schuster, 1991.

Kirkwood, G. M. *A Study of Sophoclean Drama.* Cornell Studies in Classical Philology 31. Ithaca, NY: Cornell University Press, 1994.

Knox, Bernard M. W. *Essays: Ancient and Modern.* Baltimore: Johns Hopkins University Press, 1989.

————. *The Heroic Temper: Studies in Sophoclean Tragedy.* Berkeley: University of California Press, 1964.

————. *Oedipus at Thebes.* New Haven, CT: Yale University Press, 1957.

————. Introduction and notes to *The Three Theban Plays.* By Sophocles. Trans. Robert Fagles. New York: Viking, 1982.

Lefkowitz, Mary R. *The Lives of Greek Poets*. Baltimore: Johns Hopkins University Press, 1981.

Lloyd-Jones, Hugh, trans. *Oedipus Tyrannus*. By Sophocles. Loeb Classical Library 20. Cambridge, MA: Harvard University Press, 1994.

Lloyd-Jones, Hugh, and N. G. Wilson. *Hypomnemata*. Göttingen, Germany: Vandenhoeck & Ruprecht, 1997.

———. *Sophoclea: Studies on the Text of Sophocles*. Oxford: Clarendon Press, 1990.

Moore, J. A., trans. *Selections from the Greek Elegiac, Iambic, and Lyric Poets*. Cambridge, MA: Harvard University Press, 1947.

Pickard-Cambridge, Arthur. *The Dramatic Festivals of Athens*. 2nd ed. Revised with a new supplement by John Gould and D. M. Lewis. Oxford: Clarendon Press, 1988.

Plutarch. *The Rise and Fall of Athens: Nine Greek Lives*. Trans. Ian Scott-Kilvert. London: Penguin, 1960.

Radice, Betty. *Who's Who in the Ancient World*. London: Penguin, 1971.

Rehm, Rush. *The Play of Space: Spatial Transformation in Greek Tragedy*. Princeton, NJ: Princeton University Press, 2002.

Reinhardt, Karl. *Sophocles*. New York: Barnes & Noble–Harper & Row, 1979.

Seaford, Richard. *Reciprocity and Ritual: Homer and Tragedy in the Developing City-State*. Oxford: Clarendon Press, 1994.

Segal, Charles. *Oedipus Tyrannus: Tragic Heroism and the Limits of Knowledge*. 2nd ed. New York: Oxford University Press, 2001.

———. *Sophocles' Tragic World: Divinity, Nature, Society.* Cambridge, MA: Harvard University Press, 1995.

———. *Tragedy and Civilization: An Interpretation of Sophocles.* Cambridge, MA: Harvard University Press, 1981.

Taplin, Oliver. *Greek Tragedy in Action.* Berkeley: University of California Press, 1978.

Thucydides. *The Landmark Thucydides: A Comprehensive Guide to the Peloponnesian War.* Ed. Robert B. Strassler. New York: Touchstone–Simon & Schuster, 1996.

Vernant, Jean-Pierre, ed. *The Greeks.* Trans. Charles Lambert and Teresa Lavender Fagan. Chicago: University of Chicago Press, 1995.

Vernant, Jean-Pierre, and Pierre Vidal-Naquet. *Myth and Tragedy in Ancient Greece.* Trans. Janet Lloyd. New York: Zone Books, 1990.

Whitman, C. E. *Sophocles.* Cambridge, MA: Harvard University Press, 1951.

Wiles, David. *Greek Theatre Performances: An Introduction.* Cambridge: Cambridge University Press, 2000.

———. *Tragedy in Athens: Performance Space and Theatrical Meaning.* Cambridge: Cambridge University Press, 1997.

Winkler, John J., and Froma I. Zeitlin, eds. *Nothing to Do with Dionysos?: Athenian Drama in Its Social Context.* Princeton, NJ: Princeton University Press, 1990.

Winnington-Ingram, R. P. *Sophocles: An Interpretation.* Cambridge: Cambridge University Press, 1980.

Zimmern, Alfred. *The Greek Commonwealth: Politics and Economics in Fifth-Century Greece.* 5th ed. New York: Modern Library, 1931.

ACKNOWLEDGMENTS

Translation is a thoroughly collaborative venture. The many scholars, theater practitioners, and friends who read and commented on this work at various stages deserve gratitude.

Three classicists, Thomas Fauss Gould, John Andrew Moore, and Charles Segal, did not live to see the publication of the present volume, but their influence and advice remains in the translations, introductions, and notes to the three Oedipus plays.

Mary Bagg's editing of the notes to this volume gave them clarity and accuracy they would not otherwise possess.

Thanks to the following readers for their contributions and suggestions: Normand Berlin, Michael Birtwistle, Alan L. Boegehold, Donald Junkins, Tracy Kidder, Robin Magowan, William Mullen, Arlene and James Scully, and Richard Trousdell.

Special thanks to my agent, Wendy Strothman, who saw the possibility of a complete volume of Sophocles and skillfully helped accomplish it.

ABOUT THE TRANSLATOR

Robert Bagg is a graduate of Amherst College (1957). He received his PhD in English from the University of Connecticut (1965) and taught at the University of Washington (1963–65) and the University of Massachusetts, Amherst (1965–96), where he served as Graduate Director (1982–86) and Department Chair (1986–92). His awards include grants from the American Academy of Arts and Letters, the Ingram Merrill Foundation, the NEA and NEH, and the Guggenheim and Rockefeller foundations. His translations of Greek drama have been staged in sixty productions on three continents. Bagg, who is writing a critical biography of Richard Wilbur, lives in western Massachusetts with his wife, Mary Bagg, a freelance writer and editor.

NEW TRANSLATIONS
BRINGING THE WORKS OF SOPHOCLES
TO LIFE FOR A NEW GENERATION

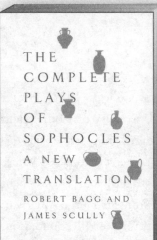

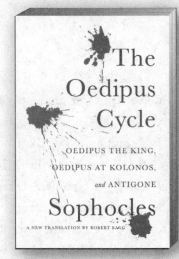

THE COMPLETE PLAYS OF SOPHOCLES
A New Translation
ISBN 978-0-06-202034-5 (paperback)

AIAS
A New Translation
ISBN 978-0-06-213214-7 (paperback)

ANTIGONE
A New Translation
ISBN 978-0-06-213212-3 (paperback)

ELEKTRA
A New Translation
ISBN 978-0-06-213206-2 (paperback)

THE OEDIPUS CYCLE
A New Translation
ISBN 978-0-06-211999-5 (paperback)

OEDIPUS THE KING
A New Translation
ISBN 978-0-06-213208-6 (paperback)

PHILOKTETES
A New Translation
ISBN 978-0-06-213216-1 (paperback)

WOMEN OF TRAKHIS
A New Translation
ISBN 978-0-06-213204-8 (paperback)

OEDIPUS AT KOLONOS
A New Translation
ISBN 978-0-06-213210-9 (paperback)

Available wherever books are sold, or call 1-800-331-3761 to order.